PLAYING BETTER BASEBALL

Rick Wolff, MA
Consultant, Cleveland Indians

Human Kinetics

Library of Congress Cataloging-in-Publication Data

Wolff, Rick, 1951-
    Playing better baseball / Rick Wolff.
      p.   cm.
    Includes index.
    ISBN 0-87322-936-3
    1. Baseball--Training.   I. Title.
    GV875.6.W65   1997
    796.357'07--dc21   96-48349
                                                                   CIP

ISBN: 0-87322-936-3

Developmental Editor: Kristine Enderle; **Assistant Editor:** Coree Schutter; **Copyeditor:** Bob Replinger; **Proofreader:** Karen Bojda; **Indexer:** Kathy Bennett; **Graphic Designer:** Robert Reuther; **Graphic Artist:** Denise Lowry; **Photo Editor:** Boyd LaFoon; **Cover Designer:** Jack Davis; **Photographer (cover):** Anthony Neste; **Photographer (interior):** Chris Brown, unless otherwise indicated; **Printer:** United Graphics

Human Kinetics books are available at special discounts for bulk purchase. Special editions or book excerpts can also be created to specification. For details, contact the Special Sales Manager at Human Kinetics.

Printed in the United States of America   10 9 8 7 6 5 4 3 2

Human Kinetics
Web site: http://www.humankinetics.com/

United States: Human Kinetics, P.O. Box 5076, Champaign, IL 61825-5076
1-800-747-4457
e-mail: humank@hkusa.com

Canada: Human Kinetics, Box 24040, Windsor, ON N8Y 4Y9
1-800-465-7301 (in Canada only)
e-mail: humank@hkcanada.com

Europe: Human Kinetics, P.O. Box IW14, Leeds LS16 6TR, United Kingdom
(44) 1132 781708
e-mail: humank@hkeurope.com

Australia: Human Kinetics, 57A Price Avenue, Lower Mitcham, South Australia 5062
(088) 277 1555
e-mail: humank@hkaustralia.com

New Zealand: Human Kinetics, P.O. Box 105-231, Auckland 1
(09) 523 3462
e-mail: humank@hknewz.com

CONTENTS

PREFACE

Dozens of how-to baseball books are available in the market place today. Not one, however, provides a simple, straightforward account of how to improve your overall baseball skills and get the most out of your God-given abilities.

Whether you're in junior high school, high school, or college, this book is designed to give you an overview of how you can best assess your talents, skills, and weaknesses, and how you can then take immediate steps to improve your game—all with the purpose of putting forth your best image to professional baseball scouts.

This book deals with much more than how to cure a batting slump or how to set up a batter. It starts at the beginning with detailed training schedules for off-season conditioning, professional tips on how to find a batting approach that suits your style, guidance about how to build your arm strength, and, of course, many inspirational examples of current major leaguers who were once your age and hoping to get a shot at pro ball.

The book takes you through every phase of the game: conditioning, pitching, hitting, fielding, base running, and the mental side of the game. In addition, an entire chapter shows you how to market and showcase your talents.

I've played and coached at both the collegiate and professional levels, and I always thought that I knew just about everything there was to know about baseball. But there is an old saying in this game that the more you stay around it, the more you learn. Believe me, it's true. It's my hope that as you go through these pages you'll discover some secrets of baseball that will directly benefit your game. After all, if there's one thing that all serious ballplayers want to do, it's play better baseball. That's the precise focus of this book.

ACKNOWLEDGMENTS

Many thanks and a tip of the cap to my wonderful and very conscientious friends at Human Kinetics who all pitched in to make this book come to life: Rainer Martens, Ted Miller, Kristine Enderle, Coree Schutter, Brian Holding, Marydell Forbes, Boyd LaFoon, and all the rest. Believe me, I know firsthand how difficult it can be to edit a sports book!

And a special salute to my friend Vin Holland, for his terrific photographic skills.

1

LEADING OFF WITH THE BASICS

"Baseball is a great, fun game. Why, it's the greatest game ever invented!"

Anybody who has ever played serious baseball will tell you that. They'll tell you of the game's inner strategies, of the amazing history, of the colorful personalities, of the pressure-filled clutch situations, and of course, about the fun of being a member of a solid ballclub. What many people can't tell you (as much as they'd like to) is how to prepare yourself to play ball at the highest level your talent will take you.

As a former player, college coach, and roving coach with the Cleveland Indians, I've seen great players waste their shot at the pros. I've seen players with less than all-star potential parlay their skills and determination into baseball careers. Of course, I've also seen great talents become great players.

Yes, there is some luck involved in getting to the majors. But you don't win signing bonuses in a state lottery. You earn them. If you're prepared to put forth the effort to master the fundamentals and to work continuously on learning advanced skills, then this book will show you how to play better baseball.

THREE TRUTHS OF BASEBALL

Let's make something clear right from the start. Baseball is different from other popular team sports—a lot different. And to underscore that reality, here are the three basic truths that I drill into young pro players all the time:

1. You have to understand—and accept—that coping with failure is a major part of the game.
2. You have to understand—and accept—that keeping your emotions in control is vital to your success in the game.
3. If you want to succeed at the higher levels, you have to understand—and accept—that baseball demands that you be well rounded and consistently able to execute a number of skills (running, fielding, hitting, throwing, and so on).

Once you come to grips with these three premises, then you can move on to the inner essence of the game, its mental and psychological side. Let's start by taking a look at the three truths of baseball in more detail.

Coping With Failure

Even though baseball is the best game ever invented, it's also the most frustrating. As the late Bart Giamatti put it, "The game is designed to disappoint you." Think of it. Basketball players score routinely, and score often, in their games. Not so in baseball. Scores of 2-0 or 4-1 are common. At the major-league level, pitchers who compile .500 win-loss records are more than decent. If you succeed merely 30 percent of the time as a hitter, you're a bona fide star.

Here's a typical example of how frustrating baseball can be. I was watching the Yankees play one evening last summer, and Tino Martinez and Paul O'Neill, two of New York's better hitters, came up to bat. Tino hit a solid line drive that the center fielder snared on the run. Then Paul laced a shot that also was caught.

The next batter was Ruben Sierra. Now, Sierra is normally a pretty good hitter as well, but he had been in a slump. During this at-bat, he was fooled on a couple of breaking pitches. Sierra finally swung at a pitch that jammed him badly, but he got just enough power into his swing that the ball looped softly over the third baseman's head. Sierra was safe on first with a squib-shot single.

What's the lesson of this story? Simple. In this one half-inning, Martinez and O'Neill both hit the ball right on the fat part of the bat, but came away with nothing to show for their attempts except 0-for-1s. Sierra, on the other hand, looked terrible at the plate, yet walked away with a base hit. You can just imagine the frustration of the first two batters—and the joy and elation of Sierra. In a nutshell, that's the nature of the game.

Controlling Emotions

Football players can take out their frustrations—legitimately—by body slamming their opponents. The same goes for hockey players. But baseball players must have a totally different perspective. Baseball demands that you keep your emotions and anger in check. Losing control only makes you and your game go downhill. Similarly, being too pumped up can undermine your baseball skills.

I've worked with numerous major- and minor-league pitchers who have told me that when they're too pumped for a game, they have control problems because they overthrow their pitches and release the ball at the wrong spot in their mechanics. Ironically, many times these pitchers tell me that they've pitched their best games when they were feeling a little tired or fatigued beforehand—when they weren't as pumped as at other times.

The state you should try to achieve is what pro coaches call *relaxed concentration.* That might sound like a contradiction in terms—an oxymoron—but that's where you want to be: neither pumped too high nor drained too low. You're simply relaxed and focused on what you're trying to accomplish in the game.

Acquiring Skills

One of the best methods for coping with baseball's high failure-to-success quotient is to acquire solid fundamental skills, to always strive to learn advanced skills, and to develop your consistency. Knowing you have solid skills to rely on will also help you keep your emotions in check when the game gets tough.

Your baseball skills evolve as you grow older. When you start out as a six- or seven-year-old, your biggest thrill is putting on that new Little League uniform for the first time. After that, it's getting your first hit, or throwing strikes over the plate and striking out a batter. Like most kids, you keep track of your batting average, and take great pleasure learning how to make plays in the field. You also enjoy beginning to get a sense for the rules of the game.

By the time you're in junior high school, you've discovered your specialization. You have a sense about whether you're a better pitcher, infielder, or catcher. You start to concentrate more on one position, although you still may like to play several different spots in the field. Offensively, you're just beginning to show what you can do. You may still experiment freely with your batting stroke as you look to maintain a high batting average or hit for more power. This is the right time to do this because your batting habits aren't fully set yet.

By the time you've reached high school, you're crystallizing in your mind what your true abilities are. This is the time to exploit your athletic gifts fully and to work on both strengths and weaknesses while pursuing your baseball dreams. This is also the time to develop yourself physically by working with weights, to study video and still shots of yourself, and to lock in on what you want to accomplish on the baseball field. If you're at or approaching the point where you've grooved the fundamentals of the game, and you're serious about baseball after high school, then this book is for you. In the chapters that follow, we'll talk about subjects that your high school or American Legion coach may not have had time to cover. We'll talk about conditioning, practicing effectively, developing better offensive techniques, learning advanced fielding skills, and getting quality at-bats. We'll go into the mental side of baseball. We'll also discuss how to market yourself so you can help the scouts or college coaches discover you.

You may often wonder exactly what it's going to take to get a look from a scout or recruiter. To know this, you need to know what you currently have to offer and what you feel you need to learn. I suggest that you put together a relatively short, written chronology of your development as a player. Start with your earliest memories of Little League and go right through your years in other organized baseball leagues. Try to mark your physical growth along with your on-the-field growth.

THE CHRONOLOGY

You can keep an accurate account of your daily progress over a season by using *Game Day*, a baseball diary for serious ballplayers. It's published by Baseball America, written by yours truly, and costs $17.95. Call 1-800-845-2726 to order a copy.

From your chronology, you'll see that you have developed substantially over the years. But there's no reason to assume that you've reached your full potential at the age of 18 or 19. In North America, ballplayers talk about someday reaching their full potential—as though their top potential was at a certain level, or peak. Once you reach that peak, so our American philosophy goes, you try to stay there before you inevitably start to slip back again. In Japan, where baseball has been the national pastime since the end of the 19th century, ballplayers see themselves as always striving to get better. They do not see reaching their potential as arriving at a certain peak level. The Japanese believe that you keep getting better and better as you practice more and more. This explains why Sadaharu Oh, the legendary Japanese home run king, continued to work at his hitting skills well into his late 30s and early 40s even though he had broken Babe Ruth's record years before; he was still trying "to reach his potential."

So don't figure you're done at 19. Too many young ballplayers tend to relax and fall off in their conditioning after graduating from high school. This is just the time to press forward more vigorously, because the key developmental years for any ballplayer are from ages 15 to 21. Not only does your body continue to grow physically and build more strength after your high school years, but you also begin to develop a stronger mental maturity about the game and what it expects of you. Remember that most major leaguers don't reach their true *physical* peak as players until they are 27 or 28.

Young players should recognize that consistency is not an inborn trait. You have to keep playing baseball and working at your game. As you might imagine, simply having the physical talent doesn't insure that you'll be consistent. Consistent performance is a by-product of practiced repetition—practice and then more practice. Keep pushing to perfect your skills.

Does practice really help? Well, consider this example. Do you recall the first time you tried to drive a car? Most people, athletes included, feel totally confused the first time they sit behind the wheel. How do you remember which pedal to push, which arm to hit for the bright lights, how to parallel park, and so on?

Even the most coordinated athlete requires some time to reach the point when driving an automobile becomes almost second nature. Similar experiences would include learning to ice skate or learning to ride a bicycle. In all these cases, certainly you have the raw physical ability to master the skills—all you need is some practice.

The same approach applies to baseball. There was a time that throwing a pitch a certain way felt awkward or clumsy, or playing a new position felt uncomfortable. But like driving a car, the more you practice, the more it becomes second nature to you. And the more it becomes second nature to you, the more consistent you become, and, of course, with consistency comes confidence. That's where, as a ballplayer, you ultimately want to be. The truly great hitters are confident; they don't worry about hitting the ball hard. Manny Ramirez, the great Indians slugger, once told me that he never troubled himself about hitting the ball hard, even when he was in the minors. "I know some other players worry about their hitting and their batting average," Manny told me, "but to me, I just know that if I get enough at-bats, I'll always hit the ball hard at some point."

That's not bragging. That's just a quiet self-confidence. When you begin to reach that level of consistency and confidence, you're on your way. The next time you go to a major-league ballpark, note how the players carry themselves on the field. They seem to exude confidence and a certain expectation of success. That expectation of success comes from the inner drive that pushes them.

MOTIVATION AND DETERMINATION

Some ask, "Isn't it the job of the coach to know how to motivate his players?"

Not exactly. The most successful coaches know that it's much easier to motivate players who are already self-motivated. In other words, the self-motivated player already knows what he wants to accomplish; his coach merely helps him channel those energies onto the pathway to success. A coach may be the greatest motivator of all time, but unless his team is already self-motivated to work hard and get the job done, his best inspirational words will be ignored.

If you think it's your coach's responsibility to push and motivate you, then you're on the wrong track. If you're satisfied with just doing the drills, with just getting by, with doing what's asked of you and nothing more, well, that's what the majority of players do—and the vast majority of players don't advance. You'll rarely find a top competitor who has done only what was asked of him and nothing more. He knows that he has to answer to himself, and usually his inner drive is more demanding than any coach.

Your Inner Drive

Joe McIlvaine, the highly talented and highly regarded general manager of the New York Mets, has said for years that the key to a ballplayer making the grade at the big-league level usually boils down not to his physical abilities, but to his desire to improve and win. "At that level, the 'mental side' of the game becomes most important," says Joe, who once pitched in the Detroit Tigers organization.

How many times have you seen a very talented player fail to win consistently or fall short of his goals? You say to yourself, "Boy, if I had that kind of raw physical talent, I'd be a superstar!" What may be lacking is the inner drive, or determination, or self-motivation to succeed. It's essential that you have both talent and drive if you want to succeed in baseball, or for that matter, in any sport or life endeavor.

That drive to succeed comes from within. You must want to work hard to improve yourself. You must dedicate yourself to doing those little things that your competition doesn't do. And that drive can't be taught or drilled into you by your coach. Either you want to get the job done, or you don't.

Yes, it might sound trite and old-fashioned, but numerous psychological studies of the best athletes show that they have two major traits in common: one, physical talent and, two, desire to keep working at their game.

To illustrate this point, take a look at the following story about one of baseball's great center fielders, Brett Butler of the Dodgers.

Your Course of Action

It's hard to believe that a star outfielder like Brett Butler was told repeatedly as a high school player that he was simply too small to play pro ball, much less play in the big leagues. When Butler was a junior in high school, he wasn't even a starter on his team. When he graduated a year later, not one college offered him a scholarship to play ball.

Butler still believed in himself even though no one else did. To keep at it, he attended Arizona State University. As a walk-on, nonscholarship player, he played on the junior varsity squad. But Brett knew he still hadn't reached his full potential, and he transferred from Arizona State to Southeastern Oklahoma State University.

Finally, Brett got the chance to play every day as a starter on a varsity program, and there he proved what he could do. He put up some great numbers. Even with all the personal satisfaction of doing well at Southeastern Oklahoma, Brett still had his eyes set on a pro career. Although that persistent label "too small" followed him, Brett was drafted. He was elated even though he wasn't picked until the 23rd round. His reward was a token bonus of $1,000.

Brett saw his dream come true—not because a coach or parent was pushing him, but because he was pushing himself. Even more important, he never lost that sense of inner confidence—the self-confidence that all great athletes carry, even when things aren't going their way.

Your Work Ethic

Again, you have to remember that not all great athletes have this inner drive. But the winners do. Coaches are always complaining to me, "I have this kid who's got more raw ability than anybody I've ever seen . . . but he just doesn't seem to care, or work hard at his talents."

What those coaches are talking about is that self-motivated push, the need to succeed that only the truly great competitors have. As I said before, it's not something that's taught or learned. It's a feeling, an emotion, a deep competitive urge that drives an athlete to reach his goals—goals that, in many cases, he's been told that he is never going to reach.

Some years ago, *Baseball America* did a study to see just how many major-league players were drafted through the traditional June draft. What surprised even the experts at *Baseball America* was that close to one out of every six ballplayers in the big leagues wasn't drafted.

Not just bypassed in the first round. *Not drafted at all!* That means that a sizable proportion of big-league ballplayers had to overcome the deep personal anxiety and frustration of sitting by the telephone on draft day and not receiving the call. After the disappointment of not being drafted set in, each of these players resolved to overcome the odds of being a nondrafted free-agent player and somehow climbed his way into pro ball and ultimately to the big leagues.

Think of it. Major league stars like outfielder Bernard Gilkey, closer Heathcliff Slocumb, catcher Jim Leyritz, infielder Mike Bordick, infielder Casey Candaele, and knuckleballer Tom Candiotti were bypassed by the draft.

I recall talking one day with knuckleballer Tom Candiotti when he was with Cleveland. Candy, who has a bright, bubbly personality, had just signed a substantial contract with the Tribe, and he was reflecting on his struggle and determination to get to the big leagues. He had been an outstanding college pitcher, but pro scouts told him that he just didn't throw hard enough to merit a professional contract. Of course, when draft day came, Tom's phone never rang.

Undeterred by this universal rejection, Candiotti talked his way into playing on a short-season independent club in the Northwest. He did well, eventually earning some recognition from pro organizations, and was ultimately offered a contract.

From there, Candiotti worked his way up the ladder, from Rookie ball to A ball to AA, and eventually to AAA and the big leagues. It wasn't glamorous, and along the way he had to overcome some serious arm problems. But here he was, standing next to me in a big-league clubhouse, feeling justifiably proud of his long road to success and financial reward. I'll always remember Candy's parting comments to me: "You know, Rick, they're paying me all this money just to play baseball, to play a sport I love. The truth of the matter is—I would have paid *them* just to have let me play."

THE MENTAL SIDE OF THE GAME

If there's one theme that keeps popping up at the higher levels of baseball, it's the mental side of the game. It's also a theme that will continue throughout this book. Just about every manager and general manager in sports today will tell you how important the mental aspect of the game is. Whether it's Joe McIlvaine (the general manager of the Mets) or Mike Hargrove (the field manager of the Indians), every top baseball man considers this a vital side of the game.

Many people—fans, owners, even some managers—like to make the mental side of baseball into something mysterious. You'll discover as you read this book that it's not. There are two separate (but complementary) aspects to the mental side of baseball: an analytical side and a psychological side. The analytical side is thinking about what to do. This means that as a player you are always engaged in the game. You have a book on the pitcher; you know what that pitcher is likely to throw you given the pitch count, the score, the inning, and which of your teammates are in scoring position. The psychological aspect of the mental side of baseball is knowing that you can execute what you've been thinking about.

When you've honed your fundamental skills, when you've learned how to think during a game, and, subsequently, when you've allowed those skills and your baseball intelligence to bolster your emotions, the result is the quiet self-confidence we've been talking about. This is a common trait that successful ballplayers have, and it's parallel to that inner drive to succeed. The ballplayers who know that they can get the job done—the ones who know that they've worked to develop and polish their skills—are the ones who develop into the best ballplayers they can be.

It's hard to pinpoint at first, but over the course of time, the player who knows that he can always throw a strike, or make that pivot at second base, or put that bunt down begins gradually to feel comfortable in his ability to play baseball at a consistent level. Want examples? Think of Greg Maddux throwing strikes, Barry Larkin scooping up a ground ball, Kenny Lofton stealing a base. They all show a quiet, professional confidence at doing their jobs. You can too.

In sum, many ballplayers can *analyze* what they should do in a game, or can figure out what the right strategy is. They can even figure out what they have to do to improve their game and their skills. But only a small percentage of players know that they can both analyze their game and then make the appropriate adjustments.

I recall speaking with Gary Ward, the legendary head baseball coach at Oklahoma State, about one of his prize pupils, Robin Ventura. Ward told me that Robin had the rare ability to listen to a critique of his batting style and then instantly incorporate the suggestions into his stance. Most players take weeks, months, even years to make these kinds of alterations in their strokes. Ventura could make changes practically overnight.

In other words, Ventura could conquer both the analytical and the psychological aspects of the game. He analyzed the problems, learned how to make the proper adjustments, and knew psychologically that he could make effective changes right away. That's the secret to both the analytical and the psychological aspects of the game.

SECRETS TO BETTER BASEBALL

What's the secret to playing better baseball? The answers are simple, and they're no secret at all. Above all, remember that baseball is a game of skill. It's meant to entertain you, and to be fun. If you truly enjoy improving your skills by practicing and playing the game, then whether you're playing ball as an amateur in a sandlot league or playing as a professional shouldn't make much difference in your enjoyment.

Second, if you do enjoy playing the game, then chase your dreams. There are very few hard-and-fast realities about the sport, but one is that you can't chase your dreams of playing pro ball if you wait too long. The clock is ticking. Chase your dreams while you're in your late teens or early 20s. That's the time to explore all avenues in pro ball.

Third, don't let anybody—coach, parent, or friend—discourage you. It's your dream—and it's your life. You be the one who decides just how far you want to go with it. As long as you have the confidence and the drive, keep pushing for it. Remember that there are many guys in the big leagues who had to overcome the same obstacles you do.

As you go through this book, you'll find tips, drills, and advice that will help you realize your potential. You may find a number of surprises: baseball myths exploded, inside dirt on how the pros really do their job, how the game is played at the top levels.

But as you read, also remember that the beauty of baseball is that it's a game that lasts for a lifetime—either as a player, manager, scout, coach, parent, or fan. Jim Bouton, the famous author and former Yankee pitcher, summed it up perfectly: "You spend a good piece of your life gripping a baseball and in the end it turns out that it was the other way around all the time."

2

USING THE TOOLS
OF THE TRADE

© Terry Wild Studio

There's just no question about it. If you want to play your best, you want to feel and look your best. To do that, it's essential that you pay more than a little attention to your equipment, your uniform, and the tools of the trade of being a ballplayer.

Now, normally, it doesn't take much prodding to get a ballplayer to understand this philosophy. Most ballplayers take their physical appearance on the field quite seriously; many spend hours in front of a mirror, preening and practicing just to get that proper look with their uniform, cap, socks, or whatever. There's nothing wrong with that. You should take pride in your uniform and your equipment.

Ballplayers instinctively know that their physical appearance on the field is the first thing that many scouts notice. Does the ballplayer wear his uniform with pride? Does he carry himself as though he's proud to be out on the field?

So, to be a complete ballplayer, you want to look like a complete ballplayer. Let's start at the bottom and work our way up.

SHOES

Twenty years ago, footwear in baseball was pretty standard stuff. Everybody in pro ball wore plain black, thin, leather spikes, regardless of what position they played or what team they played for. Once the shoes were broken in (and that took several days), these black leather spikes were actually quite comfortable. The leather was somewhat lightweight, and, like a baseball glove, they fit the owner nicely. Problem was, the shoes were still fairly heavy by today's standards, and when they got wet, they got even heavier.

These days, of course, choosing baseball footwear is more complex. The best advice to follow—and you'll hear this advice as a common theme—is to find a pair of shoes that you feel comfortable in. That means choosing a pair of shoes that you can perform in at your highest competitive standards without any pain, discomfort, or worry.

You know you're wearing good shoes when, while you're playing, you have totally forgotten them. If you are constantly aware of your shoes because your feet hurt, or you get blisters, or you can't run or move at top speed, then it's time to try a different pair. You can't be totally focused on your game if you're always fighting foot pain.

These days the typical ballplayer must choose from several types of shoes—high-tops, low-cuts, thin leather, metal spikes, rubberized spikes, all-purpose turf shoes—and, of course, among different colors and brands of shoe.

At the major-league level, as you might imagine, ballplayers have enough money to buy several different kinds of shoes. In many cases, major leaguers have contracts with shoe manufacturers that provide several free pairs for the season. Some major leaguers use certain shoes just for batting practice. Others are just for games. Some are only for playing on artificial turf. Look at any major leaguer's locker, and the first thing you'll see is several pairs of baseball shoes.

Assuming that you're not earning a major leaguer's salary just yet and that you have a restricted budget, it's important to figure out what shoes best fit your individual needs. If you're a speedster on the bases, it's important for you to wear the lightest shoe around. If you're a slugger, you might want to go with the high-top look, in the hope that you'll draw more support from this kind of shoe when you take a hefty swing at the plate.

If you're a pitcher you need to find a durable shoe to stand up to all the pushing and landing you do off the rubber. These days most shoes designed for pitchers come with a protective "pitching toe," or plate, already built into the shoe. If you see double duty as a pitcher and as a position player, it's probably worth your while to buy two pairs of shoes: one for days when you pitch and another for when you play in the field.

One word on color. Most schools, universities, and other organized ballclubs (including the pros) usually want their players wearing the same color baseball shoes. The coach makes that choice, and it's up to you to go along with it. That's just part of being a team player.

When you're buying baseball shoes, keep these thoughts in mind. Always buy your baseball shoes one half-size smaller than your regular street shoe. If you wear a size 10 street shoe, you're probably going to be fine in a 9-1/2 baseball shoe. Why? Remember that you're wearing only a thin sanitary sock with your baseball shoe and that the standard leather in a baseball shoe is much thinner than the leather in your regular shoe. The combination of both factors allows you to wear a half-size smaller. All pro players know this. If you wear baseball shoes that are too small, the toes of the shoe might curl up, not only becoming uncomfortable but also unattractive.

Whether to wear metal spikes or all-turf shoes is really your choice. Some ballplayers like to dig in intensely at the plate, and to do that, you need metal spikes. Others like playing the game in lightweight all-turf shoes. There is no real advantage to either type except that when you play on artificial turf, you'll be better off with the all-turf shoe.

Finally, keep your baseball shoes clean and dry. That's important. After each game—especially when you have played on a wet field—take a towel or sanitary sock and clean your shoes. Try to remove the excess dirt and as much moisture as you can. Keep the shoes off the floor; put them in a spot where they can dry quickly.

SOCKS

Like shoes, baseball socks have changed a great deal over the last decade. It used to be that everyone wore plain, white sanitary socks. Nowadays, while some players still wear sanis, others wear a simple pull-up sock that has the stirrup painted or stitched on the side. Others don't wear sanitary socks at all.

If you wear standard-issue white sanitary socks, you should be aware of a few points. For example, to protect yourself from developing blisters on your toes, you should wear the sock inside out. That's because at the toe of the sock, where it's sewn together, the darning causes a raised bump or lip of material. If that raised bump is rubbing directly against your toes, you might develop an irritation and perhaps a blister. To avoid that, wear the sock inside out so that the raised darning will be on the outside, facing away from your toes.

Second, many ballplayers still roll their sani socks with their stirrup at the top of their legs in the hopes of keeping both the sani and the stirrup up. If you do that, remember that with too much rolling of the sanitary sock the stirrup can sometimes cause your calf muscle to cramp up. Especially if your socks come equipped with a rubber band at the top, you can find yourself with a tired, cramped leg by the late innings of a game.

Some players wear elastic garters to keep their sanis and stirrups up. Here, players wrap the simple garters around the tops of the socks and fasten them with Velcro. This usually eliminates any cramping, but they don't always do a great job of keeping your socks up.

But again, socks have been changing. More and more players wear a one-sock combination that has the stirrup painted or sewn into it. This kind of sock eliminates the need to roll the socks up on the pant leg, and most have an elastic top that keeps them fairly stable up on the player's leg during the game. Almost all sporting-goods stores carry these socks. Buy a pair and see how you like them.

A few players don't even wear sanis anymore. These players wear their pants very low to their shoes so that all you can see is the outer sock, which has a very low-cut stirrup. These ballplayers merely wrap their feet in their low-cut stirrup and put on their shoes. Because their socks are so minimal and their pant legs are so low, there's no need to bother with a sanitary sock. Jim Thome of the Indians, for one, does this.

Finding the best look and feel for you is nothing more than a personal choice. Wear what makes you feel good so that you can play up to your potential.

GLOVES

Besides several pairs of baseball shoes, you'll find several baseball gloves in a major leaguer's locker. That's because major leaguers either have glove contracts to wear a certain manufacturer's glove or can afford to buy several different pairs. During a season, a typical major leaguer will have three gloves going at once: one, his gamer, a second for batting practice, and a third as a backup.

Of all the items you buy for your game, your glove is perhaps the most important and the most expensive. A good glove is going to run anywhere from $150 to $300 in a typical retail sporting-goods store. Just as you would try on a good suit before buying it, try on your new glove before you shell out your money. Like a good suit, that new glove should last you several seasons.

Buy a glove brand you know and trust. In the baseball world, glove manufacturers include Rawlings, Mizuno, Wilson, and others. Be wary if it's a brand name that you've never heard of. A glove that costs a few dollars less may be made from inferior leather. When you buy a new glove, it's important to take your time and make a solid investment. Once you take a glove home and start to oil it and break it in, it's difficult to return.

BREAKING IN YOUR GLOVE

There are several methods to breaking in a new glove. One of the best ways is also one of the more radical ones. Get a bucket of warm water, an old baseball, and some big rubber bands. Take your brand new glove and, yes, submerge it in the bucket of warm water. Keep it there for a few minutes to make certain it's soaked.

Don't worry. The water won't ruin the leather, nor will the leather lose its shape. The water softens the leather, and while it's in a softened state you can mold the glove to your personal needs. Place your hand inside, hammer out the pocket and shape you want, and then take the ball and place it in the pocket, just where you want it. From there, wrap the glove around the ball, and quickly wrap the glove and ball inside it with rubber bands, making it tight.

Then let the glove sit off to the side on a ledge or table where it's room temperature. Don't place it near a heat source. Within a day or two, the leather will dry. Unwrap the rubber bands, take the ball out, and work the leather some more. At this point add some Glovolium or neat's-foot oil to keep the leather soft and moist. You can even use shaving cream right out of the can. Work the shaving cream or oil right into the pocket. With a few days' use on the practice field, your new glove should be ready to go.

Some ballplayers skip the bucket of water and go right to using shaving cream in the pocket. That's fine too. But in my experience, I find that the leather responds much more quickly once it's soft and malleable from the dousing in the water.

Manufacturers add all sorts of bells and whistles to gloves these days. Inflatable fingers. Tricky stitching. Different colors. Different gimmicks. The truth is that most of these added gadgets (such as inflatable pumps in the glove) really don't add value or usefulness. What's important is whether or not it works for you.

Use baseball common sense. If you're a middle infielder, look for a smaller glove with a solid web so that it's easy to pick the ball cleanly and get it out of your webbing in a hurry. If you're an outfielder, you can use a larger glove, but make certain it's still manageable: Some outfield gloves today are just too big, and getting the ball out of the glove quickly can be difficult.

If you're a pitcher, you need a glove that's big enough to hide your pitches. Be careful not to buy one that's too small. Remember that once you pitch the ball, you immediately become another fielder. Find a glove that you can field with.

First basemen need a glove that can scoop, close easily, and be durable. Catchers, of course, want a relatively lightweight glove that can be snapped like a fielder's glove.

BATS

The first bit of advice that every Little Leaguer hears upon picking up his first bat is to "get one that feels right for you." That's still sage advice, but let's try to get a little more specific. The best bat for you is one that matches your baseball personality and needs. That is, before picking out a piece of lumber (or aluminum), first take a long, hard look in the mirror. Determine whether you're going to be a home run hitter, a slap hitter, a bunter, a line-drive hitter, or a pull hitter. If you have a difficult time figuring this out, ask your coach—he'll tell you.

From there, you can start to pinpoint what kind of bat might be best for you. For example, sluggers traditionally like to use a thin-handled bat with a thick barrel. This style of bat gives greater whip action and provides tremendous power when the barrel hits the ball solidly. The disadvantage is that the pitcher can jam you more easily; if you don't make solid contact with the barrel, you lose a considerable amount of power.

Singles and gap hitters are better off finding a bat with a medium to thick handle and a long but medium-thick barrel. The medium to thick handle helps cut down on a long, looping swing, and provides the hitter more control over his stroke. It's easier to hit the ball to all fields with a shorter, more compact stroke. The downside is that you give up a certain amount of power by using this kind of bat; however, if you're not a home run hitter to begin with, this isn't much of a sacrifice.

Also, as you might imagine, bunters are better off with a medium to thick handle and a long barrel. Such a bat gives the hitter more control of the bunting surface at the plate.

Size and Weight

This is usually an area of confusion for aspiring ballplayers. For some reason, ballplayers always assume that the bigger the bat, the more power it can generate. The reality is that power is generated by the velocity of the swing, not by the size

One type doesn't fit all: a bat for the slugger (a), singles and gap hitter (b), and bunter (c).

or weight of the bat. Let me repeat that so it sinks in: *The amount of power you generate in your swing is determined by how quickly you swing the bat, not by how big the bat is.* If you don't believe me, ask a physics teacher!

Knowing this, you can better understand that most major leaguers don't use bats much bigger than the ones found in your team's bat bag. Tony Gwynn, the premier hitter in baseball today, uses a bat that isn't much larger than 31 inches and 30 ounces. And remember that Tony stands about six feet tall and weighs over 200 pounds.

Could Tony swing a heavier bat? Sure, but as a scientific hitter and a serious student of the game, he has determined that bat control and swing velocity are the two keys to his game (remember that Tony is a singles and gap hitter, not a home run slugger).

So when you pick up a bat, find one that generates the quickest swing velocity for you. Don't be too concerned about its lack of size or weight, or even length. Most young ballplayers use a bat that's too big for their needs. Find one that suits your baseball personality and don't be too quick to give up on it.

Wood Versus Aluminum

Controversy continues about hitters making a transition from metal bats to wood bats. I've studied this topic very closely over the years. The scientific research I've read indicates that the difference between wood and aluminum is real but often exaggerated. Here's a quick summation:

Faster Jump. A ball does jump off an aluminum bat faster than a wooden bat, but it doesn't jump off that much faster. I recall reading a study in *Collegiate Baseball* that showed this to be true. But the surprising part of the study was that the ball jumped only a small fraction of a second faster off the metal bat—so little as to be practically insignificant for a high school or college player.

Jammed Pitch. If you are jammed by a pitch when hitting with an aluminum bat, the ball goes farther than it would had you been hitting with a wooden bat. This is fairly obvious; the aluminum bat doesn't break whereas the wooden bat will. All modern-day pitchers know this. They have all made a great pitch to a batter only to see him muscle a flare over the infield because the aluminum bat didn't break. That same pitch to a batter with a wooden bat breaks the bat, and the ball becomes an easy out.

It's gotten to the point where an entire generation of pitchers has stopped pitching inside to batters in high school, college, and other amateur leagues. They have learned that the aluminum bat permits this cheap hit. In any professional league with first-year pros, pitching coaches spend a great deal of time teaching young pitchers the art of throwing inside. The ability to work inside is, of course, useful to any pitcher, and it is still particularly effective against batters using wooden bats.

Simple Economics. Why do amateur players use aluminum bats? A typical aluminum bat, say an Easton or a Worth, runs $100 to $140. That's pretty expensive, but it will last several seasons without breaking or becoming dented. A good wooden bat manufactured by Hillerich and Bradsby or Adirondack runs about $30, but in a typical season one batter might break as many as six or seven bats. Some quick math easily determines that in the long run it's much less expensive for the team to buy a few aluminum bats rather than continually stock new wooden bats.

Should you be concerned about making a transition from aluminum to wood when you sign a pro contract? My personal feeling is that it's not that big of a deal—unless you make it a big deal. If you become convinced that without your beloved "metal masher" you're not going to hit well, then you will indeed have problems. But most good pro hitters will tell you that it makes little difference whether your bat is made of aluminum, wood, fiberglass, or bamboo—if you consistently hit pitching hard, you're going to hit well. It's as simple as that.

Too many first-year pros claim that a poor batting average in the pro ranks is due to the transition from metal to wood. That, to me, is really nothing but a hitter's excuse to save the embarrassment of acknowledging that amateur pitchers were easier to hit than pro pitchers. After all, many first-year pro players make the transition from aluminum to wood with no problem at all. Why don't *they* have difficulty going from metal to wood?

It doesn't hurt for you to experiment with a wooden bat every so often. During batting practice, pick up a wood bat and try it. You'll note that wooden bats always seem heavier and bulkier. Why? The aluminum bats tend to have more of their weight in the barrel of the bat, whereas the typical wooden bat's weight is more evenly distributed.

Manufacturers are constantly experimenting with new materials to make a durable baseball bat. I remember in college that we were given some bats made of compressed bamboo strips. They didn't work too well. Some of the newer ones are made of a ceramic alloy; others are a mix of chemical components. Manufacturers design them to be long lasting and to give the batter the feel of a real wooden bat.

© VJ Sports Photography

Tony Gwynn can find the gaps with the help of his bat—a thick-handled stick with a long but medium-thick barrel.

One of the most popular (and successful) chemical compound bats is made by the Baum Company. Many pro teams are using Baum bats for batting practice because they are so tough and rarely break. A Baum bat looks just like a dark wooden bat, and even sounds like one when it hits a pitched ball. The only difference that most players report is that the Baums are a little heavier than standard wooden bats. But don't be surprised if more teams start using the Baums as a cost-saving device—in both pro ball and amateur leagues.

BAT ACCESSORIES

There's nothing better for strengthening your wrists than swinging a bat. Most pro players swing a bat dozens of times a day. Even when they aren't actually swinging their bats, they're thinking about making their stroke perfect. As a developing player, you too should strive to make your swing as perfect as possible.

Batting Rings or Donuts

These heavy, O-shaped rings slide right onto your bat and help to strengthen your wrists. Quite simply, the stronger your wrists, the better a hitter you'll be. You just won't find a major-league hitter who doesn't have strong wrists.

Next time you watch a major-league game, check out the forearms of the hitters. They all look like Popeye's. The muscles and tendons right before the elbow are exaggerated in size because of the players' wrist strength—strength that players developed over the years by hard work.

Batting Tees

If you watch batting practice before any major-league game, you'll find that many major leaguers like to work off a batting tee to keep their stroke perfect and in focus. You too will find that using a batting tee is a wonderful way of eliminating from your stroke any hitches or unwanted movements. It also allows you to pinpoint what your best stroke should be.

Even more important, when you can't get outside to practice because of cold weather, a batting tee provides a useful way to practice. It allows you to lock in your stroke, day in and day out, over the course of a long winter.

Batting Gloves

It's the rare ballplayer today who doesn't use a batting glove. A generation ago, very few players wore such gloves, and if they did, it was merely to protect a serious blister or bruise on their hands.

Batting gloves are much more common these days. Most players use them primarily to get a better grip on the bat handle. Some players claim that the thin leather glove helps protect their hands from being stung during cold weather.

Protective Hand Devices

Speaking of cold weather stinging your hands, commercial devices are available that you can place around your thumb to cushion the blow between the bat handle and your hand. It's up to you to decide whether such a device works for you. Some batters like the extra protection; others find that the device merely gets in the way of their grip on the bat.

UNIFORMS

There are very few experiences as exciting in sports as getting that new uniform. Being given the team uniform is a distinct moment of pride for every ballplayer because it symbolizes that you were good enough to make the team. As such, you should always take great pride in your appearance, and in the way you wear your team uniform. If you harbor dreams of someday getting a professional contract, make certain you look good in your "uni."

Uniform Pants and Shirt

Start with the shirt first. While you want to look good, make certain that your shirt gives you enough room to throw a ball and swing a bat. On the other hand, if your shirt is too big, do what you can to get a size smaller. It's just as hard to play in a uniform that's too big as it is to play in one that's too small.

With the pants, fashion on the ballfield has changed dramatically over the last decade. Many players like the old-fashioned look in which the pants are more like knickers, ending right below the knee. Note the way Chicago's Ozzie Guillen wears his pants. Other players prefer the pant legs to go all the way to their shoes.

Again, it's a personal preference unless your team has a dress code. If your coach insists that all the players wear their uniforms in the same fashion, then obviously you want to do what he says. But most players have a preference. Some pitchers, for example, like the pant-leg-to-the-foot look because they tend to scrape their knees and shins on their follow-through off the mound. Others like this particular style because it protects their legs when they steal and have to slide on the dirt. But there really isn't any distinct advantage of one way over another.

Undershirts

Most pro ballplayers bring at least two undershirts with them to each game. They bring one that they wear under the uniform for batting practice and warm-ups before the game, and another to wear during the game.

Particularly during warm weather, when you work up a heavy sweat during batting practice, it's a good idea to take a few seconds before the game to go into the locker room and change your undershirt. If you don't, the cooling effect of your perspiration drying out your undershirt can give you a chill, and even more dangerously, cool your arms and shoulders so that you might pull a muscle.

While having two undershirts is a good idea for most ballplayers, it's mandatory for pitchers. Pitchers always break a heavy sweat when they're working. To reduce the risk of muscle injury, pitchers should change their undershirts before the game. Some pro pitchers will change undershirts every inning if they're working hard during a game.

Get in the habit of always packing a few extra undershirts in your equipment bag. And make it part of your pregame ritual to change your shirt.

Jackets

Jackets are used primarily by pitchers, who should consider their jacket as important as their glove or spikes. It doesn't matter how hot it is—any pitcher who wants to take care of his arm always brings a jacket to both practices and games.

You wear the jacket whenever you come off the field during a game. Don't wait for the coach to remind you. Have your jacket on the bench always, next to a dry towel that you can use to wipe off excess perspiration.

Without a jacket, your arm will quickly begin to cool down. Even in hot weather, this cooling action begins to take place as soon as you take your seat on the bench. To prevent your arm muscles from cooling down too much, thus risking injury, put the jacket on to keep the arm muscles warm and protected.

The jacket itself should be warm. A thin windbreaker is usually not enough. Wear a well-constructed baseball jacket that keeps the warmth within the sleeves. It should be large enough that you can put it on and take it off without strain.

Sliding Protection

No matter how talented a base stealer you are and how adept you are at sliding, chances are that at some point in the season you're going to scrape your knee or shin during a hard slide. Fields with rough, hard dirt around the bases increase the probability that you will come away with a bloody red scrape or strawberry. The problem is that once you've developed a scrape on your knee or leg, you're likely to keep tearing it every time you slide. Over the course of a season, the wound can become so painful that it can affect the way you slide.

To protect yourself, try wearing a basketball player's kneepad on one or both knees. It doesn't have to be a big, bulky kneepad, but it should offer enough protection that when your knee hits the ground no scrape results.

If you can't find a kneepad that's suitable, buy a small elastic Ace bandage. Wrap that around your knee or knees before each game, and bind it in place with white adhesive tape. Over a long season, you'll find the Ace bandage or kneepad to be of great protective value.

In the old days, players liked to wear sliding pads. These bulky and somewhat heavy pads were designed merely to protect the player's flanks from scrapes and strawberry patches. Sliding pads have gone out of style because most players today wear a pair of spandex bicyclist's pants under their uniform pants. These short pants offer the same kind of protection as sliding pads do and give you more support around the top of your thighs and groin area.

It's inevitable that during the season you're going to get a variety of bumps, bruises, and scrapes. By protecting your knees, thighs, and legs with kneepads, bandages, or short spandex pants, you will considerably reduce these nagging injuries.

Protective Cup

The protective cup is your most important piece of equipment.

Most young players don't like wearing a cup. But you might as well become used to wearing one now because it's so vital that you have one. Getting hit in the genitals is not only extremely painful but also quite dangerous. Every ballplayer can tell you a story of what it was like when he got either a bad hop or a foul tip into that area and was saved from serious injury by his protective cup. One can only shudder about what happens to players who are hit there and aren't wearing a protective cup.

Catchers, please note: Most pro catchers protect themselves by using what's known as a banana cup. Unlike the standard cup, which is triangular in shape, this kind of cup is shaped something like a banana so that it also covers the area underneath the genitals. It provides more protection from a batted foul ball that hits the ground and then bounces back up under your jock.

UNIFORM ACCESSORIES

Sunglasses first became popular for fielders about 30 years ago. The traditional flip-down sunglasses, however, have been largely replaced by darker and larger wraparound sunglasses in both pro and amateur ball.

Many manufacturers make these wraparounds; however, among pro ballplayers the Oakley brand is the most popular and probably the most expensive as well, running close to $100. No matter what brand you buy, make certain that the sunglasses are easily cleaned, made of protective shatterproof glass or plastic, and fit snugly around your head so that they don't fall off when you're running hard.

On particularly bright sunny days, some players use eye black to help reduce squinting of the eyes. Traditional eye black is a grease that comes out of a can, like shoe polish, and is applied directly on your face. Eye black, however, can become messy, especially if you are sweating profusely, and you may have to apply it more than once during a game.

More ballplayers today prefer to use eye-black patches, which are black strips of adhesive tape that are affixed under the eyes. They don't smudge or come off during the game, and they are easily removed afterwards. They offer the same eye protection as the eye-black grease.

Your baseball cap, like your sunglasses, should fit snugly so that it doesn't constantly fall off when you're running. Most caps come with adjustable bands these days, so take time to size your cap properly.

Your batting helmet should also fit snugly, but not too tightly. If you're lucky enough to have your own helmet, as all pro players do, then make certain you find the precise size for you. Remember that the length of your hair will make a difference in how the helmet fits. Keep that in mind when you select a helmet size.

One last point about helmets. Frustrated ballplayers often punish their helmets by throwing or kicking them. Remember that a batting helmet is expensive. It's also your best friend when you're batting. Think twice before you throw your helmet down on the ground or kick it 10 yards just because you swung at a bad pitch or because you were out on a close play at first.

Quite honestly, wrist bands and wrist tape rarely serve any purpose other than a psychological one. Some players claim that the bands and tape make their wrists feel stronger or more ready to swing hard. But beyond appearance, I've seen no scientific evidence that these serve any purpose.

If, however, wearing wrist bands or tape makes you feel better about your ability to get the job done, then go ahead and wear them. After all, they are popular accessories with players today, so they must serve some positive purpose.

Becoming more popular with ballplayers these days, the TMJ (temporomandibular joint) biteplate looks like a small version of the mouthguard that football and ice hockey players wear. Designed and fitted for the individual player by a dentist, the TMJ biteplate is usually used to reduce stress that occurs by an unconscious clenching of the jaws.

Some performance enhancement specialists theorize that by using a TMJ biteplate, a player can not only reduce the stress that builds up during a close game but also redirect to the neck, shoulders, and arms the muscular pressure generated by the clenching jaws. In other words, you can actually enhance your physical strength by transferring this stress-related energy to another part of your body.

If you would like to know more about the TMJ biteplate, the best place to start is your dentist. Most dentists are familiar with the plate and can tell you how much it would cost to design one for you. Be certain to ask what they have heard about TMJ biteplates helping to improve an athlete's performance by reducing stress.

CATCHER'S EQUIPMENT

Of all the positions on the field, catching has the greatest potential for causing injury. If you're a catcher, you must take good care of your equipment so that it will take good care of you.

Mask

Your mask should fit snugly, but not tight. Take time before the season to adjust the straps on the mask so that it fits properly. Make certain that the protective bars are fastened well and that the face padding is not worn down.

Remember that the mask must be sturdy. You'll be tossing it around throughout a game as you chase foul pop-ups, and of course, you'll be taking the occasional foul ball off the mask. If the mask droops down on your face or rattles too easily, get it fixed now! Don't wait until the game.

Throat Guard

This is a critical part of your face mask. Throat guards come in various sizes and shapes, but regardless of the one you choose, make certain that it is big enough to protect your throat when you have the mask on and that it is well secured to the mask. Don't chance catching a game without a throat guard on.

Shin Guards

Be certain that the guards fit you properly. Your legs should be well covered by the guards, and you should be able to run fairly easily with the guards on (when, for example, you run down the first-base line to back up first base). Be sure that the straps don't squeeze your legs too much. Again, a little preventive effort here insures that all parts of your equipment work with you, not against you.

PACKING FOR ROAD TRIPS

Of course you want to include all the basics when you go on the road, such as your uniform, jock and cup, fielding gloves, cap, shoes, and so on, but as an extra precaution, you ought to pack along

- a small towel,
- a plastic bottle of disinfectant and a packet of Band-Aids for scrapes and skinned knees,
- an extra pair of sanitary socks,
- an extra stirrup sock,
- some eye black,
- your sunglasses,
- a turtleneck in case the weather turns chilly,
- an extra fielding glove,
- your jacket,
- an extra T-shirt, and
- any other personal items you might need (such as extra glasses, or contact lenses).

Before the start of the season, jot down on a card a checklist of the items you should always take on a road trip. Keep the card in your travel bag or duffel bag all season, and check it before you zip up your bag.

DRESSED FOR SUCCESS

For better or worse, one of the components that pro scouts evaluate in a prospect is how you look in a uniform. Do you take pride in your appearance? Do you have a uniform that fits? Do you keep your shirt tucked in? Do you wear your uniform in a way that looks good? In the real world, clothes may not make the man, but in the world of baseball, your uniform can speak volumes about you.

3

CONDITIONING YOUR BODY AND THROWING ARM

There was a time in baseball, not too long ago, when ballplayers didn't take their off-season conditioning that seriously. For that matter, they didn't take their in-season conditioning seriously either!

But these days, every earnest ballplayer realizes that basic conditioning and staying in top physical shape are critical to his success in the game. If you haven't yet come to this realization, well, it's time you did. To get the most out of your God-given physical abilities, you must get serious about your body.

To that end, this chapter will offer you a brief overview of the various conditioning and weight-training programs that most professional ballplayers use to prepare themselves for the upcoming season and keep them ready during the season.

Ironically, over most of the history of baseball—right up until the 1980s—players and pitchers were always told to stay away from lifting weights. The generally accepted theory held that ballplayers didn't want or need to become too bulky in the arms. Baseball people thought that building up biceps and triceps would only cause problems for ballplayers and would in no way help them.

It was felt that pitchers and players should have only "sleek, fluid muscles" so that they could maintain and continue their "natural body rhythm and flow." Weight training and lifting would cause their muscles to bulk up too much, causing unnecessary arm, leg, and back problems.

Nobody knows who started this theory, or why. Maybe some player back in the early years of baseball hurt his arm by lifting too many barbells, thus ending his baseball career and engendering the philosophy that baseball types should avoid weight training. Today, of course, you'd be hard pressed to find any ballplayer who doesn't do at least some weight training.

Ballplayers *do* have enough sense to go about their weight training and conditioning in a smart and sensible style. Yes, it's possible to hurt your arm or back if you lift carelessly or without a planned approach. So before you start entertaining any far-reaching ideas about a weight-training and conditioning program, be sure to do the following:

1. Check with your coach. This is a must! Your coach may have a very specific idea of how he wants to approach a weight program. Make certain he knows what you're

doing, how often you're doing it, and that you're supervised when lifting.

2. If your coach isn't familiar with weight training, find an instructor or teacher in your school who is. Don't trust your friends or an upperclassman! While weight training can bring you many benefits, it can also be dangerous, so know what you're doing—and what you're trying to accomplish—before you head to the weight room.

GETTING STARTED: A SENSIBLE OVERVIEW

Because weight programs must be tailored for the individual player, most of the suggestions in this chapter are broad in scope. Several factors will influence your approach, including the following:

Your Age

The aspiring baseball player, in my opinion, shouldn't lift weights until he is at least 14. Yes, it's true that some experts on physical conditioning feel that it's fine for kids younger than that to start weight training. During these critical early teenage years, however, you're probably better served as a ballplayer by waiting until a good portion of your body's growth and development has already taken place.

Whatever age you decide to start, be certain not to rush your weight program. Go easy on the weights you lift, and don't handle too many repetitions. Pulled or strained muscles are not what weight lifting is all about!

Your Health

You should obtain a clean bill of health before you start lifting. Consider your weight, physical ailments, injuries, and health history. Check with your family physician first if you have any serious medical or physical concerns.

Your Plan

Lifting weights without a game plan won't do you any good and might even set you back. Because lifting weights is a long-range project, you should have an idea of which muscles you're trying to improve and why.

Your plan should include an attentive buddy to help spot the weights for you and help keep you on track. Lifting weights by yourself can be dangerous; always have a competent spotter with you who will pay attention to what you're doing.

A WEIGHT-TRAINING PROGRAM

Many weight-training programs are available, but I want to recommend the ones that I feel most comfortable with. From my experience as a baseball coach and player, I feel that the most beneficial programs are those that emphasize the wrist, arms, shoulders, and back. I like my players to lift three times a week, with a day off between each session, and I ask them to keep a daily chart of what they lifted, how much they lifted, and how many repetitions they performed. Such a chart allows them to track their daily progress.

Wrists

To me, the part of the body that the ballplayer should most work on strengthening is not his arm or his back or his legs but his wrists! The more you can do to increase your wrist strength, the stronger a player you'll become.

Think about it. Whether you're a hitter or a pitcher, your wrist is involved in just about every play. Coaches and scouts always talk about "wrist strength" or "quick wrists"—and unless you're just naturally born with great wrist strength, the only way you're going to secure this vital tool is by working at it.

Curling Exercises. One of the easiest ways to strengthen your wrists is by grasping a rod attached to a weight with a rope, and then trying to roll, or curl, the weight up over the rod. A good aspect of this exercise is that you don't need an extensive system of gym weights. You can manufacture this simple apparatus with an old broomstick, a weight (such as a batting donut), and some string.

To gain the maximum benefit for your wrist, make certain that your arms are level. Try to do at least 7 to 10 reps every night without stopping as you curl your wrists. Once you master 10 reps, you can add a little more weight.

Don't worry about rushing this exercise. If you're not accustomed to it, you'll find that it isn't as easy as it looks. But it's great for your wrists!

This simple exercise will strengthen your wrist and prepare you for the season. Slowly roll the donut up and down 10 times.

Squeezing Exercises. It doesn't matter whether you squeeze a manufactured hand or wrist squeezer, or just a tennis ball. Just get in the habit of doing 10 solid squeezed reps with each hand. Tennis balls are great because they're portable and easy to use.

When I was playing pro ball, I carried a tennis ball with me everywhere and squeezed it all the time. It may look silly to your friends, but believe me, if you start squeezing a tennis ball at the beginning of the school year, by the time spring arrives your wrist strength will be greatly improved.

Shoulders

One of the best ways to build up your shoulder muscles is to use dumbbells. There are a variety of routines to do with dumbbells, and all of them help strengthen your shoulders. The dumbbell bent-over rowing exercise and the dumbbell upright lifting motion are two solid examples.

As with all lifting motions, keep track of your actions on a daily basis, and don't push it too fast. Start with a weight you can handle easily and build from there.

a   b

Exercise your shoulders and prevent injury. The lifter grips the dumbbell in one hand and rests the other hand on a bench (a). The lifter's palm is facing his body and his back is straight. In the top position (b), the elbow should be slightly higher than the shoulder.

Arms

Dr. Frank Jobe, an orthopedic surgeon, is considered the world's leading expert on how to repair and prevent pitching arm injuries. He recommends a series of weight programs for young pitchers that not only increase arm muscle strength, but also cut down on arm injuries.

Side (Lateral) Shoulder Raise. The first drill involves a light dumbbell (no more than five pounds). While holding the weights in your hands at your sides, bring your hands up so that they are perpendicular to your sides. Like all these exercises, do this drill slowly and gently. Repeat eight times with each arm.

a   b

Side shoulder raise: starting and finishing position (a). Raise the arms directly out to the side of the body until the arm is parallel to the ground (b). Keep the elbows straight, but not locked.

Horizontal Abduction. The second drill for your arms has you lying on your back. Again, with a light dumbbell, bring the dumbbell up to your side so it's parallel with your body. Repeat slowly eight times.

a   b

Horizontal abduction: starting and finishing position (a), top position (b). Arms do not have to be raised any higher than parallel to the floor. This exercise works your shoulders.

a   b

Shoulder extension: starting and finished position (a) and top position (b). The arm is parallel to the ground at the end of the lifting phase.

Shoulder Extension. This time, take the dumbbell from down at your side and bring it gently back so that it's parallel with your body. This works your trapezius and lower-back muscles into shape. Repeat eight times.

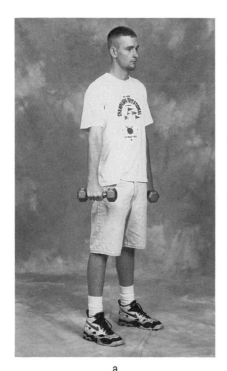 

a   b

Shoulder abduction: starting and finished position (a) and top position (b). The arm is raised
directly out to the side of the body until it is parallel to the ground.

Shoulder Abduction. The third drill has you back on your
feet and lifting the same dumbbell from your side with your
arm straight out. This is particularly good for your shoulder
muscles. Repeat eight times.

PLYOMETRICS

The science of plyometrics is relatively new to baseball, and only
a few pro organizations use it. When I was with the Cleveland
Indians as a roving instructor, spring-training sessions would
devote an hour or two each morning to plyometric drills and
skills.

These drills involve everything from sprinting around cones
(to build agility) to lifting and throwing a heavy medicine ball
(to build body strength) to doing short sprints (to increase
quickness). A complete plyometric drill session consists of

numerous exercises that individually may not seem like much but taken together develop into a hefty workout.

The goal of plyometrics is to develop and strengthen the entire body, sharpen quickness, and build stamina. Donald A. Chu, PhD, a recognized expert in this field, points out that the term *plyometrics* comes from Latin derivatives and literally translates to "measurable increases." It's an ideal way to combine strength training with speed of movement, all with the purpose of producing power.

While there are a variety of plyometric drills to choose from, Dr. Chu recommends the following plyometrics for baseball players. The good news is that the only real piece of equipment you need (other than shorts and sneakers) is a medicine ball, which is routinely found in high school or college gyms, or at health clubs.

Torso Exercises

The best way to keep your rib muscles and general midwaist muscles trim and in shape is by using a medicine ball. A

a   b

Side throw: Swing the ball to your side (a) and then forcefully reverse directions and release (b). You may toss the medicine ball to a partner or against a wall.

plyometrics approach with a medicine ball is perhaps the safest, and most effective, way to accomplish this.

Side Throw. Take the medicine ball from one side of your body, bring it around, and throw it away from you. As mentioned above, this drill strengthens your torso and improves the quickness of your torso's muscles. Toss the ball from one side of your body and then the other.

Overhead Throw. This time you lift the medicine ball directly over your head, take one step forward, and throw it hard away from you. This is good for your torso, thighs, and shoulders.

a   b

Overhead throws with medicine balls work upper and lower body simultaneously. Lift the ball overhead and behind your head (a) and then step forward and bring the ball quickly forward with both arms (b).

a   b

Lateral jump with two feet: Stand with feet shoulder-width apart. Swing one leg across your
stationary leg (a) and then bring it back to the side (b), jumping sideways as far as possible.

Lateral Jump With Two Feet. Standing straight up with feet
apart, bring one foot back and attempt to jump as far as you
can from your stance. This drill develops quickness. Do this
over the course of 30 yards. Start from a flat start, jump, and
then jump again.

Standing Long Jump. As you would guess, start in a crouch
and then long jump from a standing position. Do this over the
course of 30 yards also.

Alternate Bounding With Single-Arm Action. Standing
straight at first, bound forward on one foot using the opposite arm for balance. Bound then onto the other foot, with
the other arm for balance. It's an exaggeration of your basic
running motion; try to bound (jump) a decent distance with
each leg.

Give yourself 30 to 40 yards of open turf to execute this drill.

Plyometrics work to increase speed and decrease reaction time. Using a big arm movement (a), jump forward as far as possible (b). Land with both feet together (c).

a

b

c   d

Alternate bounding: Jog to start the drill and to increase forward momentum. This exercise is an exaggerated running action. First push off with one foot (a) and bring the leg forward, keeping the knee bent and parallel to the ground (b). At the same time reach forward with the right arm. Switch legs and arms (c-d).

WORKOUT SCHEDULE: PLYOMETRICS

For these five drills (and others like them), you should put together a standard plan of exercise. The drills shouldn't take much time; you can do them on a nearby field.

Week One

	Day				
	1	**2**	**3**	**4**	**5**
			Repetitions:		
Side throw	3	3	3	3	3
Overhead throw	3	3	3	3	3
Lateral jump	2	2	2	2	2
Long jump	3	3	3	3	3
Bounding	3	3	3	3	3

Week Two

	Day				
	1	**2**	**3**	**4**	**5**
			Repetitions:		
Side throw	4	4	4	5	5
Overhead throw	3	3	3	4	4
Lateral jump	2	3	3	3	4
Long jump	3	3	4	4	4
Bounding	3	3	4	4	5

Week Three

	Day				
	1	**2**	**3**	**4**	**5**
			Repetitions:		
Side throw	5	5	6	6	6
Overhead throw	4	4	5	5	6
Lateral jump	4	4	5	5	5
Long jump	4	4	5	5	5
Bounding	5	5	6	6	6

After three weeks, these plyometric drills should become familiar and comfortable to you. (For more information, read Dr. Chu's book *Jumping Into Plyometrics*, Human Kinetics, $13.95)

AEROBIC EXERCISE

Aerobics, which involves full stretching of the body's muscles, is a wonderful way to work out. You can use the principle of running and stretching in place to get in shape for baseball.

No, you don't have to wear leotards, but you might learn something from one who does. When I was coaching at Mercy College, I brought in an aerobics instructor to get my players into shape. I'll never forget it. The ballplayers thought it was a joke. For the first 15 minutes of the exercises—complete with blaring music—they were laughing and joking with each other.

But after a while, as the humor wore off and the sweat began to flow, the players didn't have the energy to keep laughing. By the time the class ended some 45 minutes later, the players were exhausted. They had no idea that this kind of workout was so demanding.

I had tried aerobic training because so many of our players had suffered leg muscle strains and ankle injuries from all the running we did early in spring training. In an attempt to cut down on those injuries, I introduced aerobics. Sure enough, all those preseason leg injuries disappeared, plus my players got into tip-top shape.

For your conditioning program, especially if you find running laps to be boring, try getting in the habit of doing high-powered aerobics. Most high schools and colleges offer these programs on a regular basis. For your needs, just get your best rock 'n' roll album on your tape machine, crank up the volume, and go to work dancing. Keep dancing at a good pace for at least 30 to 40 minutes. Don't worry; you'll be enjoying yourself and getting yourself into shape at the same time.

ANKLE WEIGHTS

In an attempt to build up their leg muscles, some players strap on ankle weights. The athlete wears these weights, which vary from two to five pounds, throughout the day.

I have no problem with ankle weights. I myself wore them as a kid to build leg muscle and speed, and I found that they worked for me. Just don't wear them when you're working out. Wear them when you go to class, but take them off at baseball practice. Of course, you can wear them in the evening, but remove them when you go to bed.

For players who want to develop an extra step of quickness, ankle weights certainly are a move in the right direction. Wade Boggs wore ankle weights to develop his foot speed when he was in his late teens and early 20s, and they certainly helped him.

I should point out, however, that not every expert in conditioning agrees that ankle weights are effective. Some say that using ankle weights is counterproductive because instead of building quickness, they force ankle and leg muscles to slow down. They feel that you're teaching your legs to move more slowly rather than more quickly.

So, proceed with caution. See whether you like them. If you don't feel and see an improvement within a few weeks, then you should reconsider using them.

CONCERNS ABOUT PLAYING OFF-SEASON SPORTS

The biggest fear about sports in the off-season is that you'll hurt yourself and that the injury will get in the way of your baseball career. And some of this fear is well justified: Jim Lonborg, once a top pitcher for the Red Sox, jeopardized his career when he seriously hurt his leg in a skiing accident.

But that being said, I'd rather have my players doing something physically active during the off-season than just sitting around, hoping not to get hurt. Almost any sport that involves aerobic activity is a good one. If you enjoy basketball, tennis, swimming, or racquetball, then by all means, take the necessary precautions (like wearing a pair of goggles to protect your eyes) and go have fun.

On the other hand, you might want to think twice about the more physically challenging sports, such as football, wrestling, or ice hockey. In fact, some pro teams strictly prohibit their players from taking part in such off-season activities. Too much of a concern? Just remember that Bo Jackson might still be playing baseball today if he hadn't seriously injured his hip while playing pro football.

At the other end of the spectrum, just playing golf or going bowling in the off-season will not keep you in tip-top physical shape. In other words, don't be a couch potato in the winter; get off your butt and stay in shape!

READY TO GO TO WORK!

The chapter has provided a brief survey of what pro ballplayers do these days to get and stay in shape. Weight training, plyometrics, and aerobics (running) are all a vital part of any serious ballplayer's regimen. The good news is that you don't have to spend a great deal of time on these drills every day. The bad news is that if you don't, then you won't be able to perform at your fullest potential.

Is this glamorous work? No, it's not. But it's a major part of paying the price if you want to become a top player. Every pro will tell you that they go through this process.

So, keep at it, stay disciplined in your daily approach, and during the season you'll see your hard work pay off in major improvements for yourself. It's as simple as that.

4

PRACTICING TO YOUR MAX

Let's plan out the next year in your life as a baseball player. Take out a calendar for the next 12 months. First, pinpoint the start and finish of your baseball season. Next, mark on the calendar the period of your off-season. Finally, record when your preseason practice and conditioning usually kicks in.

In this chapter, we'll concentrate on those three segments of your upcoming baseball year. In much the same way that a builder uses a blueprint to construct a house, you'll need a blueprint, or well-organized plan, to help develop your strengths and overcome your weaknesses as a player. Smart ballplayers know this intuitively, and they put together a personalized game plan on how they're going to use each part of the year to make themselves better. You should do the same.

OFF-SEASON PRACTICE AND CONDITIONING

While most fans believe that baseball players work hard during the season, knowledgeable coaches and players know that the real work of preparation, conditioning, and practice is done in the off-season.

For most aspiring players, the off-season runs from early October to the end of January. That's about four months' time in which to reflect and focus on your game—where you have been, and more important, where you want to go. The surprising part in all this is that so few ballplayers really have a solid approach to their off-season practice plans. Tossing a ball around occasionally, or swinging a bat, or lifting a few weights just doesn't get it done. Don't be one of those players who figure that because they've worked hard during the season, the off-season is a time to kick back, relax, and just hang out.

Years ago, ballplayers did exactly that. They used the off-season as a time to get away from the daily pressures of the game for a while. Once the season ended in the fall, these players didn't work out or stay in shape during the winter. They figured that spring training would give them ample time to get in shape.

As a result, until the 1960s and 1970s, many pro ballplayers would report to spring training out of shape and overweight, with the idea that they would gently work themselves back into playing shape by the start of the season in April. After all, spring training usually lasts from late February until the first week of April. That's about six weeks to get back into condition.

In most spring-training camps today, however, the coaches are eager to get going on the first or second day. That means they want to time you doing sprints, exercise you, and have you field, take batting practice, and pitch. The coaches assume that if you're serious about your career, then you've stayed in shape over the winter and are ready to rock and roll when you step into camp.

Players who aren't in shape fall behind right away, having to nurse blisters on their feet, ease muscle strains, and take care of other general aches and pains. Some never catch up. They end up being released or cut.

So start with the assumption that you want to stay in good shape all year round. Getting heavy or becoming slovenly in your off-season conditioning isn't going to get it done. Besides, all your opponents and competitors *are* staying in shape; don't make the mistake of giving them an edge.

The good news is that the off-season gives you ample time to evaluate and analyze your game. During the season you have to concentrate on the games. The off-season, without the pressure of day-to-day performance, permits you to make substantial progress in your game.

To help you organize your off-season practice schedule (and that's just what it is), you should sit down and put together a well-organized plan of attack. Here's what I normally suggest to minor-league ballplayers:

Be Objective About Yourself

Before you can implement your plan of attack, you have to be brutally honest with yourself about your game. Most ballplayers don't like criticism, but as you plan out your off-season, you must be honest and objective with yourself.

If you struck out too many times last season, or didn't run the bases well, or didn't throw enough strikes, or whatever, now is the time to list them on a sheet of paper. Trying to ignore your shortcomings, or trying to rationalize them, isn't going to make you a better ballplayer.

Remember that your list is a private matter. You don't have to show this list to anyone, and you shouldn't. But in exchange for that privacy, you have to be candid with yourself.

Now, once you have listed your weaknesses, take just as much time to list your strengths. After all, it's just as important to recognize the things you do well. Otherwise, you'll begin to lose sight of them, and those strengths won't develop.

Make a Report Card

Here's a sample "report card" that a young ballplayer might put together in the off-season:

Weaknesses

1. I guess at too many pitches at the plate.
2. I strike out more than I should.
3. I'm not very good at bunting.
4. I'm fast, but I don't steal many bases.
5. I sometimes make careless errors in the field.

Strengths

1. When I make contact, I hit the ball hard.
2. I have good bat control and can hit to all fields.
3. I get a good jump out of the box.
4. I have a good, solid arm in the field.
5. I get clutch hits.
6. I'm a thorough team player and make the plays when it counts.

Your list, of course, will be different, but remember to be objective. Try to be fair and honest with yourself about your abilities. Few players are terrific in all facets of the game, and it's rare to find a player who's terrible in all aspects.

Once you have graded yourself out with this year-end report card, you can start to formulate your personalized off-season game plan. That's an important step to success.

Review Any Visual Materials You Have

By visual materials, I mean any videotapes or still photos of yourself in action from the previous season. These days, determined players can usually engage a parent or coach who can take videotape of the player in action. Such materials can be a vital teaching tool.

HOW TO USE VIDEOTAPE TO YOUR ADVANTAGE

When your coach or parent videotapes you, keep this in mind for optimal viewing:

• If you're a pitcher, the best view of you is from behind the catcher. From that viewpoint you can get the best idea of how you, and your pitches, look to the batter. At some point get some shots of you from behind first base when you have a man on first. This will give you an opportunity to see what you look like to the runner, how easy (or difficult) it is to get a good jump off you, and just how good your pickoff move is.

• If you're a batter, the best view of you is from the side. A side-action view guarantees you'll have a chance to watch all your moving body parts in action. You can see your stride, feet, hands, weight shift, shoulders, and head. Watch the tape several times, focusing on different components each time through.

First, just run the video a few times to enjoy watching yourself play. Go back and get a sense of how you carry yourself, how you look, the image you project, and so forth. Then, after the initial wonderment has worn off, you're ready to evaluate objectively and learn from the tape.

Bring a notepad. This is homework, just like homework you do in school. Take notes on both the good and not-so-good performances. Let's say you're watching yourself hit. Find an at-bat when you did well. Look for those precise, particular aspects of your hitting form that work for you. Write down on your notepad everything about your stroke: how you held the bat, how wide your stance was, what kind of bat you used, the degree of your crouch, where you stood in the box, what kind of pitch you hit, and so forth.

Take your time doing this because your notes will help form a mental vision of what you did well when batting. That mental vision is something you want to impress upon your brain's memory throughout the off-season.

Take a few moments to go through some of your poorer at-bats. Pinpoint the weaknesses: where you hitched, or where you dropped your back shoulder, or if you lunged at the pitch, or if you were jammed, whatever. Again, take notes—see if you can find a pattern to your weaknesses.

When you've completed your homework assignment (and this video session might last close to an hour), you should come away with a highly detailed list of what you do when you're hitting (or pitching) well. You should also have a list of what you do when you hit or pitch poorly.

Prepare Your Own Mental Cue Card

Using your notes, you can now begin to digest the keys to your successful performances by listing them on an index card. Take your time, and be as specific as possible. That index card, what I refer to as a "mental cue card," is your personalized blueprint on what you have to do to succeed in baseball. It's going to be with you for the entire off-season.

Suppose, for example, that you're a right-handed pitcher. After studying videotapes of your performances (both good games and mediocre games), you reach these conclusions:

Hitters should do the same analysis. By the time you've done your homework with the video, you should have a fairly complete mental cue card that works just for you. If you follow all the steps on your cue card, then you should have a successful performance on the field. Your brain knows specifically what you're trying to accomplish.

"But who needs to write this stuff down?" you might protest. "Isn't all of this just based upon instinct? And besides, whoever forgets how to hit or to pitch?"

First, over the course of a season, many players tend to forget their personal blueprint for success (these lapses are usually known as slumps). And second, although a great deal of hitting and pitching depends on athletic instinct, you first must have a thorough understanding of what you're trying to accomplish before you can actually do it. Just hoping you'll become a better bunter won't get it done; you need a solid plan to learn how to bunt properly.

When I'm Pitching Well . . .

1. I'm on the rubber, with feet spread slightly. I face the batter squarely.
2. I have a minimal amount of motion in my windup and delivery. There's no wasted motion.
3. My right arm always comes past my head in a solid, three-quarter slot. I don't drop down to sidearm or come directly over the top.
4. I tend to drag my right knee on the mound as I follow through, getting a little dirt on the kneecap.
5. When I finish up, my feet are parallel in position, ready to field my position.

When I'm Pitching Poorly . . .

1. I find myself walking around on the mound, looking at the fans and coaches.
2. My right arm tends to slip down to the side occasionally. I do this a lot when I become tired or frustrated.
3. I don't get enough push off the rubber; I don't scrape my knee at all. As a result, my pitches usually go too high in the strike zone.
4. If the ump misses a call, I have a hard time concentrating on the next pitch. I have difficulty keeping my anger under control.
5. When I follow through, I sometimes fall off the mound to the side.

Videotapes aren't always better than still photos. While videotape is a great instructional tool, there's something to be said about viewing still photos, or stop-action shots, of yourself. Stop-action shots allow you to see exactly how you're gripping that curveball, or exactly how high you're lifting your front leg when you stride. Again, if you can afford it, ask your coach or a parent to break out the camera and take some shots of you in a game—batting, pitching, leading off, fielding, whatever.

Will it help? Before he was tragically killed in a boating accident a few years ago, Steve Olin was a terrific relief pitcher for the Indians. There was a time in Steve's career, however, that he found himself struggling on the mound. The submarine-style right-hander suddenly found that his fastball wasn't moving or dipping around the plate.

Panic-stricken, Olin worked for hours with his pitching coach, endlessly searching videotape for some mechanical difference that may have affected his pitching style. But as much tape as they viewed, it didn't appear that Olin was doing anything differently.

With no movement on his fastball, Steve feared the worst. Sure enough, his fears came true: Opposing hitters battered his offerings about the ballpark. Within a few weeks, the Indians shipped Olin back to Colorado Springs, then their top minor-league affiliate.

Upset and fearing that perhaps his major-league career had come to an abbreviated end, Olin was lounging one day in the minor-league clubhouse when he happened to pick up a baseball card of himself. The photo on the card was one of Olin in action, in mid-delivery. The more that Steve looked at the card, the more he realized that he found a key to his pitching success.

Clutching the card in his left hand, Olin grabbed his glove and ran down to the bullpen. He studied the card, trying to

© VJ Sports Photography

Steve Olin reviewed a still photo and found his fastball again!

emulate exactly how he held the ball in the still photo, and he started to pitch. Within minutes, thanks to that simple still-shot baseball card, Steve had put his career back on track. His fastball had regained its movement.

What Steve had seen in the baseball card photo was a stop-action shot of how he held the ball precisely before he released it. What happened? Unlike the videotape, which is a blur of fluid movement, the stop-action still photo allowed him to pinpoint the mechanical flaw that had caused his fastball to flatten out.

The lesson here? Yes, you should try to internalize those personalized cues or keys that indicate when you are performing well. The sooner you commit those items to memory, the sooner you can learn how to make adjustments in your game. Having a firm grasp of what works for you, and knowing how to achieve what works for you, is what the game of baseball is all about—making adjustments.

Develop Your Visualization Skills

Over the years you have no doubt heard about visualization, but perhaps you wondered what it was or whether it worked.

Visualization is a form of self-hypnosis that psychologists routinely use in all kinds of applications. Musicians, actors, public speakers, and many top performers like to "see" themselves in action before they actually go out and do it. In the sports world, it's primarily employed as a tool to help top athletes reach their highest level.

The concept is fairly simple. If you can train your mind to see yourself performing well, then you can achieve a better focus and better concentration on achieving those goals. From an athlete's point of view, that means being able to see yourself (in your mind's eye) throw strikes, or swing without a hitch, or make the plays in the field that you know you can make. At best, you can take your game to a higher level of consistency. At worst, you develop more confidence in your abilities. In sum, it's a technique that you ought to consider using.

Every night, or during a quiet time in your day, take about 15 to 20 minutes to lie down on your bed. It should be very dark; close all the drapes, and don't let in any light. There should be total quiet (no music).

Lie on the bed and close your eyes. Start by taking several deep breaths. Hold the air in and then slowly let it out. Do this at least 12 times. This process will slow your body down and relax you.

When your mind and body are relaxed, and always with your eyes closed, start to focus on the task at hand. See yourself on the baseball diamond. Envision yourself in as much detail as possible—in full color, in uniform. Take note of the other details—weather, your teammates, the coach, the opposing team, and so on. It's important to paint an entire panorama in your mind's eye.

Now, see yourself during the game. Just as though you were watching yourself on television, watch yourself do all the things you *want* to do: throw perfect strikes, sharp curves, baffling change-ups, and so on. Or, if you're hitting, hit pitches that look big to you at the plate. There are no hitches in your stroke; curves don't fool you. You're hitting solid line shots all over the ballpark.

Do everything just as you would like. *Do not* show any scenes of your struggling or failing. You must see yourself doing well.

Keep this up for at least 15 minutes, watching your own personalized highlight film. When you're done, you'll notice as you rise from the bed two things: (1) You'll feel refreshed and ready to go, and (2) you'll probably notice an adrenaline rush of excitement. That shows how your mind can truly control your body. Even though you've just been lying in bed, physically doing nothing, your mind's eye convinced your body otherwise; you'll feel as excited as though everything really did just happen.

Finally, you must get into this practice of visualization as part of your daily routine. Don't do it haphazardly. You must do it as a regular part of your practice routine. When you get into a real game situation, you'll find that your performance anxiety will have lessened dramatically. Why? In your mind's eye, you've already faced this scene of action many times before. What was once anxiety-provoking now becomes routine. That's the beauty of visualization.

Prepare Your Daily Workout Chart

Now that you have done a thorough job evaluating your past season and what you want to work on for next year, you can start planning your daily off-season workout program. You should design a program to fit your specific needs (based, of course, on your strengths and weaknesses). The program should include a full conditioning program (weight lifting, running, and a daily regimen to strengthen your wrist, regardless whether you're a hitter or pitcher). Your program should also include a visualization exercise to keep your mental vision on the right track.

As I said in the last chapter, physical fitness, conditioning, and weight training for baseball players is much different from what it is for, say, football players. In baseball, you're much more concerned with developing power for the long haul, for the long season. In terms of power, you don't want to bulk up; you're interested in lean, sinewy muscles.

In any event, here's what an off-season program might look like for a young minor leaguer who's serious about his career:

SIX DAYS EACH WEEK

- Jog two miles; finish with four 50-yard sprints. Total time: 20 minutes.
- Lift weights (as outlined in chapter 3). Time: 30 minutes.
- Practice your "perfect" batting stroke in front of mirror; take 100 practice swings, ideally with a weighted bat. Or, if you're a pitcher, practice your "perfect" delivery in front of a mirror. Use a weighted baseball in your pitching hand. Time: 20 minutes.
- Specialized drills. Work on special parts of your game that need attention (such as your pivot footwork, your move to first base, and so forth). Time: 30 minutes.
- Visualization skills. Do this at home, away from the practice field. Time: 20 minutes.

THE SECRET TO OFF-SEASON SUCCESS

The purpose of such a rigorous program is not just to keep you in shape. That's important, of course, but the real purpose of these personalized sessions is for you to concentrate on making your strengths stronger and transforming your weaknesses into strengths.

If, for example, you have difficulty putting down a sacrifice bunt, this is the time of the year to analyze your approach, correct your bunting style, and develop it into a strength. Like all learned motor skills, bunting is just a matter of practice. The more you practice the right skills, the more it becomes a reflex action—and that's where you want to be.

If you're efficient, your workout session will run no more than two hours, tops. You should repeat it six times a week. On the off-day, do only the visualization and mirror work. Squeeze a tennis ball or some other wrist strengthener whenever you have a free moment during the day.

YOUR OFF-SEASON WORKOUT SCHEDULE

Use a chart like this to track your daily progress throughout the off-season. You'll be amazed at how quickly the days go by when you chart your progress.

	Day 1	Day 2	Day 3. . .Day X
Jog/run			
Weights			
Specific work			
Extra work			
Visualization			

Under each day you should mark down just how much you accomplished. For example, if you jogged two miles and ran five sprints, note that on the chart. *Specific work* involves those skills you need to practice every day, such as swinging a bat, or working on leads and steals, or fielding. *Extra work* refers to those parts of the game which you know have been a weakness for you in the past.

By keeping track of your everyday effort, you'll begin to develop a sense of confidence about every part of your game—even those so-called weak parts.

Obviously, you can tailor your program to fit your needs and desires, and some baseball coaches have programs for their players to follow in the off-season. But this should at least give you an idea of what many pro players try to accomplish in the off-season by conditioning and staying in shape.

You should have a daily calendar in which you can mark down what you accomplish in each workout session. All athletes like to keep track of their achievements, and there's no better way to feel good about yourself and what you've done than by keeping such a calendar. Write down on the calendar your times for running two miles, the weight program you've completed, and what you worked on in your special drills sessions.

PRESEASON PRACTICE AND CONDITIONING

Around the end of January or early February, ballplayers traditionally start to get antsy. The winter days are beginning to become a bit sunnier, a bit longer, and ballplayers find themselves itching to get on the field.

The long off-season conditioning program can now be modified to include batting practice, fielding practice, and pitching or throwing practice. Keep in mind that you should not ditch the off-season program at the end of winter; rather, it should serve as a transition to your preseason workouts— a continuation and transformation of your reflective, analytical work of the winter to action during spring training.

Do you remember the time you spent visualizing yourself throwing more strikes, taking better leads, or getting around faster on the inside pitch? Do you remember the time you spent running, lifting, and practicing in front of a mirror? Do you remember all the goofy comments people made about your always squeezing a tennis ball in class?

Well, now is the time to start watching all that work pay off!

Ready to Compete for a Job

Pro ballplayers know that spring training is the time to win a job. That's when the competition is the toughest. Therefore, when they report to camp, they're already in midseason form. You should plan to be too. View your preseason conditioning program as a transition to your being in tip-top game readiness. In other words, you want to be at the top of your game on Opening Day.

All that being said, you don't want to surge so much during preseason that you pull a muscle, develop painful blisters, or burn yourself out. Stick with the basics of your off-season conditioning program, but start to mix in some live action. Preseason training is also the time when ballplayers begin to work out together. Usually, in the off-season, ballplayers tend to work out on their own, or perhaps with just one teammate. But in the preseason, ballplayers start working out in groups of six or eight.

Here's a basic but effective preseason workout routine, broken down for both pitchers and position players.

Pitchers

Running. Pitchers can now start to build endurance by running at least two miles. Ideally, pitchers should run three or four miles. You can run two miles at the beginning of practice, and then two more miles at the end. A pitcher is only as good as the endurance and stamina in his legs, and there's no better way to build your strength than by running.

Stretching. After you have finished jogging, your body should be fairly loose and warm. This is the time to stretch fully your legs, arms, and body. Take a few minutes to stretch out; in some cases, those muscles really haven't been stretched since last season.

Some of the best stretching exercises include those discussed in the previous chapter. Be certain to review the prescribed exercises involving weights, dumbbells, and gradual movement.

Calisthenics/Plyometrics/Aerobics. Whatever program you use, or your school uses, you should give yourself a good workout. Calisthenic programs usually involve the repetition of typical exercises, such as jumping jacks, toe touchers, and so on. Plyometrics (as discussed earlier) involve a series of drills, all using motion, usually in some competition against other players. Aerobics involve quick motion and movement over an extended time.

It doesn't really make much difference in the long run what system you prefer, as long as you select one style and stick with it. Just don't start with one system, stop, try another, and then go back again. Stick with one program to get maximum results.

Throwing. Often overlooked as part of your workout, throwing should not be viewed as a warm-up but as a major part of your conditioning. Start about 25 feet from your partner and gradually begin to move farther apart.

While throwing, you should be consciously working on your balance, your aim, your arm being stretched to its fullest, and your velocity. Honestly, the only—and best—way to strengthen your arm and improve your aim is to work on it in just this manner. Like hitting, your throwing can improve tremendously, but only if you work at it.

Pitching Mechanics. After you've thrown, you can start to work on fine-tuning your pitching mechanics. During preseason, you should review all aspects of your pitching. In one practice session, you can work on breaking off the mound to cover first base. In another session, you can work on your move from the stretch. Work on fielding bunts the next day.

In the meantime, you should also start a very slow progression toward pitching at full velocity. Start with throwing only 10 pitches on day one. On day two, throw another 10 pitches. On day three, go to perhaps 15 pitches. That's it. Even though you'll be tempted to throw much more and much harder, you have to be patient and careful.

Throw only fastballs at this point, absolutely no breaking stuff. Your arm isn't ready yet. Depending on how your arm feels, you slowly build your stamina. Your goal is to build your arm strength *gradually*. You normally have six or seven weeks of preseason to train. That gives you plenty of time to build up to, say, 100 to 110 full-speed pitches.

By week three or four, you can start to mix in some breaking balls. By that point in your conditioning, your arm will be ready for it, but not sooner.

PRESEASON WEEK-BY-WEEK CHART FOR PITCHERS

Week 1—Stretching, running, work on mechanics, pickoff move, fielding, very light tossing.

Week 2—Stretching, running, mechanics, pickoffs, fielding, more light tossing.

Week 3—More of the same but now you can work off a mound, throwing no more than 20 to 25 fastballs.

Week 4—More of the same but now you can start to add breaking pitches to your daily routine. Don't rush it!

Weeks 5 and 6—More of the same but you should be building up more stamina with your pitches. Aim toward the start of the season and design each workout as though you're almost in midseason form. Work off the mound as though you're in a real game situation.

Preseason Pitching to Batters. For the first few weeks, facing a batter won't do you (or him) much good. By week three or four, you can start to simulate a game situation, although you'll still be throwing mostly fastballs to the batters in a cage.

This is the time to start working hard on your control. Don't worry about being hit hard; this is only practice. And don't waste your allotted pitches. Make every pitch count; make every pitch a strike. That's how you get in the habit of throwing strikes in a real game.

To improve your control, mentally select a specific target on the catcher. Don't settle for just throwing the ball down the middle of the plate. Instead, pick out his left kneecap or his right shoulder. Lock in your mind a visual image of that specific target and then try to hit it with every pitch.

This will get you accustomed to seeing several targets at the plate (for example, outside corner, inside corner, low and away, and so forth). You'll find that the more you concentrate on a particular target, the more control you'll have. Too many pitchers concentrate on their control only during games; as a result, they don't develop the consistency they need to throw strikes all the time.

Studying the Video. If you can arrange it, set up video cameras to tape yourself in workouts. This is an excellent way to monitor your progress and see how you're achieving your goals. The best shots, of course, are those either from behind home plate, to see how you appear to the batter, or from first base, to see what work your pickoff move needs. Give yourself enough time to review your videotapes at the end of each practice so that you get a clear mental picture of what you want to work on the next day.

Position Players

Running. All position players should start their practice by running two miles and then cooling down their long jog by doing five to eight 40- or 50-yard sprints. The long jog gets your legs into shape, but remember that baseball is a game of quick starts and sprints. This is the best way to start working on those skills.

Try to work on your sprints as though you were taking a lead off first base. Work on sprinting toward second or third. You might as well get in the habit of stealing bases right now.

Stretching and Calisthenics/Plyometrics/Aerobics. This is the time to work hard on your conditioning. Position players, like pitchers, must take this part of the regimen seriously every day.

Throwing. Again, take the time to work on your throwing arm. Practice your aim, strength, and various types of throws (over the top, sidearm, three-quarters, and so forth). As you catch the return throw, get in the habit of trying to get the ball out of your glove quickly. An infielder, especially, must develop quickness with the ball.

Batting Tees. All hitters should work off a batting tee in every workout *before* they take batting practice. Working off your mental cue card, concentrate on making your visualized thoughts become real actions. Perfect your stroke off the tee.

Most batters find that working off the batting tee helps develop a Zen-like approach to hitting. Because you can focus so clearly on what you want to accomplish, you find yourself getting to a point where you know exactly what you have to do to hit the ball solidly every time.

Make the batting tee an everyday part of your training regimen. Most pro ballplayers do this so they can work from their swing blueprint every day before they start hitting off live batting practice.

Batting Practice. Take your time. Position players, like pitchers, have no reason to rush matters. Start with all fastballs off a machine, with pitches coming in slowly. Spend the first week or two concentrating on your stance and swing. Just worry about making contact—nothing else.

By the end of week two, you can start to add a little more velocity, but again, keep things under control. The idea here is to perfect your stroke, not show off to your buddies how far you can smash a 75-mile-per-hour fastball.

Then, at four weeks, you can make the transition from machine to a live pitcher. You'll see mostly fastballs, but have the pitcher occasionally mix in a curve or change.

During this time, you should also focus on the other aspects of hitting, namely bunting, the hit-and-run, and hitting to all fields. Bunt and bunt again until you feel confident that you can put a bunt down anytime, anywhere. Work on the hit-and-run until you know that you can do it every time.

I'm convinced that most hitters don't develop these skills simply because they don't practice them enough. Nobody wants to put down a sacrifice bunt, so very few players practice it. It's the same with hitting to all fields, or the hit-and-run. Since most players simply want to swing away, they don't give enough practice time to learning these vital offensive skills.

Fielding Drills. While you're waiting for your turn in the batting cage, take some ground balls. Just as you do when hitting, take time to review proper fielding position (knees bent, butt down, hands and glove out in front).

Here are a few basic exercises to try when working on your fielding in the off-season and preseason:

1. Pickups. Have one of your buddies simply roll grounders to you from only a few feet away, first to one side, then to the other. Pick up each grounder and toss it

back to him as he rolls another to you. Within five minutes, if you're doing this drill properly, your inner thighs will be burning. That's good—it means your legs are getting into shape.

By the end of the second week, you should be picking up grounders and throwing them across the gym or field to a teammate. Again, the trick here is to focus on your style and grace—not on showing off your arm strength.

A simple pickup drill like this gets your legs in shape.

2. Side-to-side extenders. Once your legs are in shape, you can try this exercise on a wooden gym floor with your socks. Get down in your fielding stance and then glide from side to side, left to right, and back again, repeating 10 times.

This exercise gets you in the habit of keeping your legs bent and your butt low to the ground, and of course, it aids tremendously in building your range from side to side. Just be careful that you are fully loose in your legs

a   b

Do this exercise and develop your side-to-side range. Get down into fielding stance (a) and slide back and forth in socked feet (b).

and groin before you start. You don't want to pull a muscle.

3. Quick release. If you're an infielder, make a concerted effort to get the ball out of your glove quickly and into proper throwing position. I have found that one of the better ways to develop quick, soft hands in this drill is to use a tennis ball when fielding in the gym, or during the off-season or preseason. Because tennis balls are so bouncy, they force you to develop pliable hands and quickness in handling the ball. Better yet, if you happen to muff a ball or two during this drill, you don't run the risk of hurting your fingers.

PREPARATION FOR GAME SITUATIONS

Toward the end of preseason practice, you should be hooking up with your teammates on turning pivots, covering bunt plays, taking throws from the catcher, and, if you have room, handling cutoffs and making relays from the outfield.

One last point about preseason. Make certain you find time to read or review the rule book. I'm always amazed that so many experienced ballplayers don't know the rules of the game. If you can't recite the infield-fly rule, or don't know which runner is out and which one is safe when both runners are standing on the same base, then take a few minutes to review the rules. You'll be amazed at how much you'll learn about the game.

IN-SEASON PRACTICE AND CONDITIONING

Many players make the mistake of assuming that once the season begins they can forget about physical conditioning. That's a major misassumption.

At any professional ballpark during the season, long before the crowd arrives for a 7:00 or 7:30 game, you'll find pitchers doing their running, perhaps at 3:00 or 4:00. Well before batting practice starts, hitters are working off batting tees and stretching.

Early Work

Routinely, in the minors and majors, ballplayers show up for "early work," which takes place at 10:00 in the morning. This could consist of special sessions to work on fielding drills, extra hitting, or whatever, and lasts about two hours. Then the ballplayers can go back to their rooms, have lunch, and rest up before reporting back to the clubhouse around 4:00 to get ready for that night's game. On other days of the week, ballplayers do their weight lifting and training under the guidance of the team's weight coach.

So, while it may appear to the casual fan that the typical pro ballplayer just shows up at the ballpark at 6:00 or so for a three-hour game, the reality is that dedicated ballplayers work hard at their craft and their conditioning throughout the season.

Running/Jogging

For your in-season conditioning, the first person to check with is your coach. Talk to him about what he expects you to do during the season. Some coaches have their players run sprints after each game; others want their pitchers to run foul line to foul line before games.

Listen to your coach. Get his advice and then do what he wants you to do. If you want more after that, tailor and adapt your program to your needs as you did in off-season and preseason training. For example, the wrist-strengthening program can certainly continue right through the regular season. There's no reason to stop that vital exercise program.

The same applies to running sprints. You can do those right after each game, running in the outfield. Start at the foul line and run 40 yards at a full sprint into the outfield. Stop, turn around, jog back to the foul line, and then do it again. Try to run at least 10 hard sprints after each game, and you'll find that your wind conditioning will stay sharp.

If you're a pitcher and prefer to jog, then you should do your running on a regular basis as well. If you run before a game, make certain it's a game in which you won't be pitching. If you can't be certain, do your running after the ballgame. Two miles should be enough to keep your legs in top shape.

Weight Training

During the season, the best time to lift is either after the game or on an off-day. Most pro players lift after the game, never before. Why?

When you do heavy lifting, a natural chemical compound called lactic acid builds up in your muscles. It takes your body several hours to drain lactic acid away from your muscles. There is no way that you can be at your peak performance level when your lifting muscles are still soaked in lactic acid; you just won't have the strength you normally have.

Remember, weight lifting should emphasize repetition, not bulk lifting. You're looking for results through repetition, especially during the season. Don't risk pulling any back or shoulder muscles by lifting too much.

Video Training

Don't forget to review your tapes every week. You should continue to track your progress at the plate or on the mound by viewing your video. Look for the cues that are essential to making your performance top notch.

If you see that you need to make adjustments, write down those thoughts. Acknowledge them. Focus on them in practice.

If you have to tinker with your movements at the plate, get out the batting tee and work in front of the mirror. The same advice applies to pitchers. Work in front of that mirror. Try to visualize the adjustments you want to make and make a mental note of them.

Finally, be certain to consult your mental cue card before each game. Take a few quiet moments in the clubhouse before each game to review carefully your personalized formula for success. Review each tip slowly; see yourself doing those things in a game. Remember, the more you can visualize yourself performing properly in a game, the closer you're getting to making those visualizations into reality.

THE GAME-READY PLAYER

Today's aspiring ballplayer takes his conditioning seriously—and tends to stick with it all year round. If you follow the preceding suggestions, you can divide your year into three parts—off-season, preseason, and in-season. True, each part of this regimen places strenuous demands on you, but in the long run, the conditioning, training, and visualization exercises will pay off handsomely. Even better, you'll be on your way to developing the inner confidence you need to become the best ballplayer you can be.

5

DEVELOPING AN OFFENSIVE ARSENAL

Al Goldis, regarded as one of the smartest men in professional baseball today, has held important positions with several clubs; most recently, he serves as director of scouting for the Cincinnati Reds. Before that, Al held similar jobs with the Chicago Cubs and the Chicago White Sox, where he was credited with having drafted and signed such stars as Frank Thomas, Jack McDowell, and Robin Ventura, among dozens of others.

"When I watch a high school team take batting practice," says Goldis, "it's amazing to me that seemingly every kid on the team tries to hit home runs, or at least swing for the fences. I don't understand that. After all, it's one thing if you're the biggest player on the team, and you're blessed with raw size and pure power. But if you're an average or below-average size ballplayer, why are you wasting your time trying to hit homers?"

Kenny Lofton hits grounders to take advantage of his speed.

© Anthony Neste

Goldis explains that it's up to you—the individual player—to take a long, hard look at what you can and can't do. "If you have great speed but don't have much power, that's OK," says Goldis. "Try to tailor your game to emphasize your strengths. Look at what Kenny Lofton has learned to do in the game to make himself great. That is, if you have outstanding speed like a Kenny Lofton or Lance Johnson, you should be learning how to swing down on the pitch, to hit grounders and line drives rather than lofting fly balls that are going to be caught. You should be learning the strike zone very precisely, so that you can get on base via walks. You should be learning how to bunt for a hit—again, so as to take advantage of your innate speed. These are the tools that are going to propel you to the next level in baseball, but sad to say, only a fraction of the kids I see in high school, junior college, and college understand this concept."

So when it comes to figuring out how to make the most of your offensive skills, you should first determine what your body size, physical strength, and limitations will allow you to do. Many coaches at the pro level call this playing within your limits.

TAKE A GOOD LOOK AT YOURSELF

As a young player, how do you determine how to play within your limits—to play within your strengths and weaknesses? That's easy. Just look around at your teammates and then at yourself. Ask yourself these questions: How fast am I? How much power do I have? Would I better serve the team (and myself) by trying to hit doubles and singles, or should I just swing for the fences? Am I a good bunter? Do I have a good eye at the plate? Can I hit the ball to all fields?

When going through this self-examination, try to be a pro scout yourself. Remember, scouts evaluate players in two ways: One, they rate how good a prospect is now, and two, they rate how good a prospect is going to be in a few years. Seeing into the future is all but impossible, but that's what scouts have to do.

To accomplish that, scouts may look at your parents or older siblings. Maybe you're a late bloomer. Maybe your adolescent growth spurt hasn't occurred yet. Of course, if you grow an extra three or four inches over the summer, everything about your game could change. Scouts know this; you should too.

Allen Watson is a hard-throwing pitcher who has played for several major-league teams and stands six-feet-four-inches tall. He's one of the better hitting pitchers in the majors. To look at Watson today, you'd never guess that he wasn't very tall when he was in his late teens. In high school, he stood well under six feet. He didn't start to grow until his senior year, and then he continued to grow right through college.

What does all this mean to you? It means that the sooner you understand and accept what your God-given athletic gifts are, and the sooner you work hard at them, the better off you're going to be. And remember that your body size and strength will ultimately dictate just where your talent lies in baseball.

BASIC LAWS OF HITTING

If you play baseball long enough, you will hear dozens of theories on how to hit a baseball. There's the Ted Williams theory, the Charley Lau way, the Walt Hriniak way, the Rod Carew way, and on and on. These theories all have one thing in common. For certain hitters they work. Sadly, for others, they don't.

The challenge is to figure out what works for you—and figure it out relatively early in your career. Don't worry, though. You can jump to the head of the class when you start taking a more calculated and educated approach to hitting.

As we'll discuss, there isn't a perfect stance in baseball. True, there are certain accepted conventions on how to stand at the plate, but so many great players have used diverse stances that it's difficult to say there is one precise way to do it.

Specific universal laws of physics, however, form the core of every good hitter's swing. More precisely, these "laws of baseball physics" include the following:

1. Your maximum power comes not from your arms and shoulders but from your legs.

    You've heard about keeping your weight on your back foot, that your back foot is your source of power. That's true. Once you launch your stroke, the strength from your back leg is transferred to your front leg, and it's transferred while you're making the contact with the ball. That transfer of power is what drives your swing and what drives the ball off your bat.

Take a moment to watch any big-league power hitter. You'll see how he stays on his back leg until he starts his swing. (Note to pitchers: What you want to do is get that hitter to transfer his weight too quickly. Once he does that, he loses his power base. You can do this by changing the speed of your pitches.)

2. To get maximum impact, hit the ball with your arms fully extended.

If you make contact with the pitch and your arms aren't fully extended, then you're not getting full power into the swing. This is similar to being jammed with a

Check out Mark McGwire's swing—fully extended arms as he makes contact with the pitch.

pitch, and you know what limited power you generate when you get jammed.

Take a look at hitters like Frank Thomas or Mark McGwire. When they make contact with the pitch, their arms are fully extended from their bodies, which gives maximum power to their swings.

3. Keep your head and eyes steady and level when watching the ball to the plate.

   Too many young ballplayers keep their head and eyes somewhat tilted or on a slant when they hit. This may sound obvious, but if your head is tilted even a little bit, the task of hitting a baseball becomes much more difficult. Be certain you face the pitcher with your eyes level and straight.

4. In general, the fewer moving parts in your swing, the purer your swing will be.

   If your swing doesn't have any hitches or pumping action and if your bat isn't moving around your head,

Ken Griffey Jr. is a pure hitter with a "clean stroke."

A compact stroke gives Jeff Bagwell power.

then chances are you're in an excellent preparatory position for hitting. Of course, some big leaguers have hitches or other moving parts. Examples include Cleveland's Carlos Baerga and Manny Ramirez. But for the most part, the genuine pure hitters are very "clean" when it comes to their strokes. Look at Toronto's John Olerud, Texas' Will Clark, Seattle's Ken Griffey Jr., or Tony Gwynn of San Diego. All these great hitters are known for their pure swings.

5. The shorter your stroke, the more time you have to wait on the pitch.

This is a universal truth about hitting, no matter your stance or stroke. Common sense tells you that the longer you can wait on a pitch before deciding to launch your swing, the better chance you have of swinging at a good pitch.

So, if your stroke is relatively short and quick, then you have the luxury of waiting a few milliseconds longer than the hitter who has a long, sweeping swing. Power hitters, because they tend to uppercut the pitch, generally have long, sweeping strokes. To get around on fastballs and to extend their arms, they must start their swings earlier. That also means that upper cutters are more likely to be fooled by curves, sliders, and splitters, and, as a result, they tend to strike out more.

On the other hand, hitters who have shorter strokes (and who tend to hit down on the pitch) are more likely to wait longer, see the pitch more clearly, and be tougher to strike out. While they might not hit as many home runs as power hitters, they're going to hit for a higher batting average and will most likely spray hits over the entire field.

Some hitters who have short strokes also hit for power. Jeff Bagwell comes to mind. He holds the bat relatively close to his ear, has a short stroke to hit for a high batting average, but has enough power to hit homers as well.

6. Remember that power is generated from bat speed—not from the size of the bat you swing.

This law follows from the one before it. Many young hitters don't understand this concept. It's not how heavy or how big your bat is—it's how quickly you swing it.

You'd be surprised to discover that many professional hitters don't use bats any heavier than the ones that college kids (or even high school kids) use. Pro hitters know that the faster they swing the bat, the harder they hit the ball. And the harder they hit the ball, the farther it will go. That's just basic physics in action on a ballfield. It's also why hitting coaches tell you to use a bat that feels comfortable. Use one that allows you to generate tremendous bat speed. That's the key to making the pitch jump off your bat.

Now, working within these six basic laws of hitting, you can make any personalized adjustments you want with your stance, stroke, and so on. But if you study big-league hitters long enough, you'll come to the conclusion that these six laws are constant throughout the world of baseball.

Finding Your Proper Stance

To me, the most scientific approach follows along these lines. First and most important, find a stance at the plate that you're comfortable with. Many of baseball's great hitters had very unusual stances:

- Hall of Famer Stan Musial used his peekaboo stance.
- Rod Carew hardly held the bat in his hands. It just sort of drooped from his fingers.
- George Brett practically lunged into every pitch.
- Roberto Clemente stood very far from the plate and dived into the pitch.
- Julio Franco of the Indians wraps the bat practically around his head before he swings.
- Ruben Sierra, another pure hitter, lifts his front foot high into the air before he swings.

Ryne Sandberg has a more traditional swing than some other great players.

- Carlos Baerga seems to change his stance on every at-bat—whether he's batting righty or lefty.
- Reds first baseman Hal Morris seems to walk into every pitch before he swings.

None of these top hitters had what you would call a standard, or classic, way of swinging a bat. I'll bet that if any of these great hitters had shown up at a batting clinic as a youngster with his unusual style of hitting, the instructor would have told him to change his stroke and stance.

So as you develop your stroke, recognize that there is no perfect stance. If there were, everybody would use it. From there, go back to your strengths and limitations.

Developing Bat Control

Are you a power hitter built like, say, Cecil Fielder? It wouldn't make much sense to get Cecil to choke up and spray the ball to all fields or work on bunting for a hit, would it?

© Anthony Neste

Use your build as a way to determine what kind of hitter you are. If you are built like Cecil Fielder, concentrate on developing a stroke with maximum power.

So if you're built like Cecil, you ought to concentrate on developing a stroke with as much power as possible. That means learning to keep your weight back on your back leg, learning how to maximize your power, and learning how to hit change-ups and curves.

At the other end of the spectrum, let's say you're built more like Lance Johnson or Rey Ordonez—thin, wiry, and quick. Guys like Johnson and Ordonez learned a long time ago that their chances of hitting many home runs in the majors were pretty slim, so they've adapted their strokes to hit sharp line drives. Fly balls hit by medium- to smaller-sized hitters are pretty to watch, but they end up being routine outs.

Becoming a Switch-Hitter

Being a switch-hitter is a wonderful advantage. The sooner you learn how to hit from both sides, the better you'll become as a hitter. True, it feels funky and goofy at first, but stay with it. If you can develop this skill, it makes you infinitely more valuable as a player as you go up the ladder. In addition, you won't ever have to deal with nasty curveballs or sliders.

Most kids try switch-hitting but give up on it too soon. They complain that it's awkward and quit after only a few days of trying. Give yourself an entire season. You don't have to try it in a game until you're ready, but you ought to go through a whole year trying it in batting practice. Like anything else in life that's new to you (remember there was a time when you couldn't even ride a two-wheeler), learning how to switch-hit takes time and patience. Ask any major-league switch-hitter if it came easy. He'll tell you that he wasn't born a switch-hitter. He had to work at it, and so will you.

The best way to become accustomed to your new stroke is by taking ball toss (see later) every day. Take at least 10 rounds of 12 pitches from both sides of the plate every day by having a teammate or coach lob pitches to you while you hit them into a screen.

Beware of Counterproductive Batting Practice

At the start of this chapter I wrote about making the most of your God-given abilities as a hitter. Batting practice is the time to identify your abilities and refine your approach to the game.

Let's consider the typical batting practice session. Sessions usually start with a few bunt attempts, and then the coach tells you to swing away. The problem is that the vast majority of young players think that batting practice bunts are nothing more than a chance to adjust to the velocity of the pitch; whether they put down a good bunt or have good bunting mechanics is irrelevant.

Most young hitters then hit away by simply taking their hardest whacks at the pitches. They try to hit the ball over the fence, swinging from their heels in an attempt to impress their coach, their teammates, their friends, or just themselves.

As a result, the typical batting practice session for most kids not only wastes time but is downright destructive. Such sessions work *against* what they're trying to accomplish. Have you ever noticed that there's very little correlation between how you do in batting practice and how you do in a game? This is especially true if you're trying to hit home runs in batting practice when you really should be working on spraying the ball to all fields.

The truth is that batting practice takes a tremendous amount of self-discipline. After all your work with the batting tee, practice swings, and soft toss, batting practice comes closest to simulating a game situation. Naturally you just want to whack away at the ball. Of course, you forget that in a game situation you're not going to have straight, half-speed pitches thrown to you.

That's why it's essential to make batting practice a work situation, not a time to show how far you can hit a ball. Use batting practice to get your eyes and hands ready to see the ball and hit it wherever it's pitched.

YOUR APPROACH TO HITTING: ONE HUNDRED STROKES A DAY

After you analyze your strengths as an offensive player, you can start to develop a precise game plan for yourself. You should have a definite idea about how you approach each game, especially with your hitting. The sooner you fall into a regular pattern of game preparation, the more comfortable you'll become at the plate.

Game preparation doesn't start with your walking up to the plate in a game and thinking about getting a good pitch to hit. It starts months earlier, during the off-season when you don't have the pressure to perform in a game situation. Too many junior high school and high school players don't realize that; they're under the impression that if they're good, all-around athletes, they don't have to work on hitting until spring training begins.

Major leaguers will tell you that you have to keep working at your stroke on a daily basis. That means refining and practicing your swing at least 100 times a day, all year round. The more you get—and stay—in that groove, the easier it will be to focus on the pitch in a game. You'll worry less about your stroke because by that time it will have become second nature to you.

If possible, practice your 100 swings in front of a large mirror or some other reflective surface. Be careful; you don't want to smash anything by accident. One of the best ways for you to become adept at self-analysis is watching yourself swing.

This is the time to get the wrinkles out of your stroke. If you have a slight hitch, the off-season is the time to eliminate it. If you shift your weight too soon, this is the time to make adjustments in your stroke. If you're trying a new stance, this is the time to perfect it.

One last thing. Try using a weighted bat to develop your wrist and arm strength. But be careful. Don't use a bat that's so heavy that it weighs down your stroke or affects the way you swing. If your off-season bat is too heavy, it will alter your swing, and that's not good.

Batting Tee: Major Leaguer's Best Friend

Because major-league ballparks usually don't open to the public until about an hour before game time, the typical fan doesn't have a chance to see that many big leaguers hit off a batting tee into the big protective screen that's behind home plate.

Albert Belle uses the tee just about every day, at around 4:30 before a 7:00 night game. Same with Don Mattingly and dozens of other big leaguers. It's part of their pregame preparation, and what it does is allow each player to maintain his groove for that night's game. Again, it's part of the preparation that goes with taking your game seriously.

When you use the batting tee, remember that you're using it to perfect your stroke. This is an extension of your 100 practice swings, except now you're swinging at an object. Because you have to replace the ball on the tee every time you hit it, this exercise puts a little more pressure on you to focus on each swing and make it count.

If you make poor contact with the ball, or if you hit the tee, it's a good indication that either you're not concentrating or there's something wrong with your stroke. Get to the point where you're making solid contact with the ball every time, hitting line drives straight ahead.

If you aren't doing this on a consistent basis, then stop and analyze. Make the appropriate adjustments in your swing. Common sense tells you that if you aren't getting it done with a batting tee, there's little chance you're going to get it done in a game situation.

Soft Toss: The Next Step

After using the batting tee, professional hitters like to add a new element into the mix—trying to hit a moving ball. In soft toss, you stand in front of a batting screen and a teammate, squatting off to your side, lobs balls so that you can hit them hard into the screen. This easy-to-do exercise is another great way to practice your hitting stroke.

Soft toss allows you to take a series of swings, perhaps as many as a dozen, in quick succession before you start becoming tired. This series of swings is an excellent way to simulate a typical at-bat in a game. If you do soft toss properly, your feeder lobs balls to you at different heights so that you first must see the pitch and then make the appropriate swing adjustment.

Many kids practice soft toss by having the balls thrown at the same spot every time. That's OK to start, but the more

Practice hitting a soft toss, but remember to vary the spot where the ball is tossed.

efficient way is to hit the pitches at different spots—high, low, inside, and outside.

Again, this is the next logical extension beyond the batting tee, because now you are being forced to concentrate on a "pitch" and swing hard. And yes, soft toss is just as popular with major leaguers as the batting tee. Everybody does it.

WHEN YOU CAN'T TAKE PREGAME BATTING PRACTICE

Sometimes, with high school or college games, there isn't time for pregame batting practice or the field is too wet to hit. Use soft toss to replace batting practice. It's an excellent way to loosen up, get the kinks out of your system, and prepare for the upcoming game.

DEVELOPING BAT CONTROL

When your coach tells you to hit away during batting practice, you should begin with your hit-and-run stroke. That means, of course, that you're going to hit that next pitch—no matter where it's thrown—to the opposite field.

By doing so, you accomplish two things. One, you learn to focus on the pitch (because you have to hit it), and two, you practice waiting on the pitch as long as you can before swinging. Both are excellent ways of making that first hit-away in batting practice worthwhile.

On all subsequent pitches, you should concentrate on two points—hitting the ball where it's pitched and hitting the ball hard. If you can do that, then you're making the most out of batting practice.

What this means is that you're waiting on the pitch and not giving in to the temptation of trying to pull everything you see. Remember, slower pitching tempts batters to pull everything with power. In a game, the greater velocity of the pitch and the variations you see on the ball (curves, sliders, change-ups, and so on) mean that you have to wait until the last moment before you decide to swing. That takes patience, self-discipline, and a practiced ability to hit the ball where it's pitched. That's what you've been trying to accomplish in batting practice—if you did it the right way.

FIVE O'CLOCK HITTERS VERSUS GAME-TIME HITTERS

Perhaps you've heard the expression that so-and-so is a five o'clock hitter. That means that he looks good when he takes batting practice at 5:00 before a game that begins at 7:00. He's the guy who strokes shot after shot in batting practice, but come game time, he looks bad at the plate—swinging at bad pitches, being fooled, and sometimes lunging at pitches.

As you might imagine, there are countless five o'clock hitters in this world. Everybody looks good when they know what pitch is coming and it's coming in slow. What you want to be is a hitter who knows how to perform in a game situation. You want to be a gamer.

To become a gamer, you have to start developing a prehitting routine for yourself that helps you focus on the upcoming game and what you want to accomplish at the plate. During batting practice, you can laugh and chat with your teammates. Hitting pitches in batting practice should be fun and relaxing. But as game time approaches, the best hitters use rituals or routines to help focus on their goals and eliminate outside distractions.

Put it this way. In a typical nine-inning game, you'll probably get only four or five at-bats. You must concentrate fully on each of these at-bats to maximize your offensive performance. Most pro players will tell you that if you hit the ball hard twice every game, you'll end up as a .300-plus hitter.

That seems like a reasonable goal, one that you should strive for. To that end, your pregame batting ritual should consist of the following:

1. Review mentally what you want to do at the plate. Remind yourself to stay on your back leg, or not to take so many pitches, or to turn on the pitch, or whatever mental cues you have worked on during the off-season. Do your review 15 or 20 minutes before the game, when you have a moment of quiet time to reflect on your batting goals for the game.

2. Once you're in the on-deck circle, you have a perfect opportunity to watch the opposing pitcher. Visualize yourself batting against him. See his motion. Check his velocity and his breaking pitches. Note where you pick up the ball off his delivery.

3. See what's working for the pitcher. Put yourself in his shoes. If he's bouncing curves in the dirt, chances are he's not going to throw you many curves. Study his pitch sequence. Does he normally throw a fastball over the middle of the plate for the first strike? If he does, be ready and look for it. The more you know about the pitcher, his stuff, and how he works, the easier it will become for you to bat against him. There's an old saying

in baseball that the more a batter sees of a pitcher, the easier it is for the batter to hit him. Now you know why.

4. Do your final mental review as you approach the plate. Take your final practice strokes and check with the third-base coach for any signs, but once you dig in, let your mind go clear.

Yogi Berra once said, "You can't hit and think at the same time." It's absolutely true. When you're waiting for the pitch in the batter's box, you should be thinking only of the pitch and whether it's a good pitch to swing at. If you're worrying about your back leg, your back elbow, your batting average, or anything else, it means that your brain isn't totally focused on the incoming pitch. Any kind of distraction is going to affect the execution of your swing.

I once asked Jim Thome, the hard-hitting third baseman of the Indians, what he thought about when hitting. Said Jim: "When I'm in the on-deck circle, I think about a lot of things— my approach, what the pitcher's throwing, and so on. But once I'm in the batter's box, I don't think about anything. Just see the ball, see if it's a good pitch, and swing at it."

In other words, after all the weeks and months of rigorous preparation, once you're in the batter's box, you have to let your raw athletic instincts take over. It's time to trust your body, brain, and eyes and let them go to work.

Some players refer to this process as "Letting go and letting God." This is the belief that once you've done your homework and have prepared for the moment, it's time to let go of yourself and let God take over. It's good, sound advice.

Trust your body during the game. Trust your instincts. Learn to trust your physical abilities. You can work all you want on polishing and refining your stroke before and after the game, but during the game, let your body take over—especially at the plate. That's the only way you can learn how to hit.

THREE LITTLE WORDS: MAKE THE ADJUSTMENT

As you go higher into serious baseball, you start hearing coaches, managers, and scouts talk about how certain players can "make the adjustments" that are needed during a game. A player who can make adjustments is able to recognize how to get the job done *during the game.* That requires maturity as well as athletic ability.

Here's an example. If, during a turn at-bat, you find yourself constantly swinging late on pitches, you must recognize that you have to be quicker with your swing. To do that, you have to make an adjustment, whether it's choking up on the bat, swinging a bit earlier, or standing deeper in the batter's box.

Scouts and pro coaches look to see just how quickly you can make that adjustment. Will it take you several at-bats during a game? Just one at-bat? Or just a couple of pitches during the same at-bat?

The quicker and sooner you can make that adjustment, the better a ballplayer you'll become. Baseball is really a chess game played with muscles, and making those adjustments are what it's all about. Of course, learning how to make adjustments takes time. Few amateur players can make adjustments quickly. Learning how to do so requires time and patience.

Some ballplayers elevate the art of making adjustments into a science. Mike Hargrove was a .300 hitter in the majors for years. Dubbed the "human rain delay" because of all the time he took between pitches, what he was really doing between pitches was quietly analyzing his last swing and making adjustments in his head. Mike knew how to make adjustments that quickly—on a pitch-by-pitch basis.

Most other top-flight hitters are the same way. Tony Gwynn can make slight yet significant adjustments on a pitch-by-pitch basis. So can Robin Ventura. And on and on. The point is that the sooner you know how to make adjustments in your swing or in your delivery, the better and more consistent you'll become.

A WORD ABOUT SUPERSTITIONS

I personally have no problem with a player having superstitions if he really thinks that it will help his performance, and if his superstition doesn't get in the way of another player or offend the team or a teammate.

Superstitions are psychological mechanisms that a player employs to stay in a particular groove. You usually see a player develop a superstition when he's doing well, as though there's some sort of cause-and-effect relationship between two events.

Let's illustrate how these things happen. For example, a player says to himself that ever since he started using his lucky brown bat, he has hit the ball hard. So, from that point on, the player uses his brown bat in every game. He continues to hit well, and by the end of the season, he's convinced himself that it's his lucky brown bat that is responsible for his good hitting.

Looking at this chain of events a little closer, it becomes apparent that the player's brown bat was a little lighter and easier to swing than his previous bat. As a result, he had a quicker stroke. With a quicker stroke, the player hit the ball harder and ultimately got more hits. This is a more plausible explanation of the player's success at the plate, but all he sees is the new bat and the higher batting average. Hence, the superstition begins to build.

This is a simplistic example. But if you start looking at behavior among ballplayers by considering that they look for cause-and-effect relationships between events, then you'll develop a better idea of what's going on in their heads.

There's a fine line between a superstition and a preperformance ritual. For example, Wade Boggs always eats chicken on the day of a game. To outsiders, that may seem odd or superstitious behavior. But for Wade, eating a meal of chicken provides peace of mind about the upcoming game and allows him to relax just a bit more.

Is this superstition or merely a preperformance ritual? If you asked Boggs, he'd tell you that superstition has nothing to do with his dietary habits. It's just part of his pregame preparation. And judging from his career batting average, who's going to argue with him?

What's the bottom line on all this? Simple. If you have developed pregame preparation rituals that give you an inner peace or calm or confidence, then there's no reason you should modify them. Just understand and accept that if your performance begins to slip, you might want to look more deeply at what works for you and what doesn't as your pregame performance rituals.

THE SECRET BEHIND BUNTING

Everybody in baseball says that players can't bunt because they don't work at it anymore. Or they say that kids can't bunt because they play with aluminum bats, or that kids don't want to bunt because they want to hit home runs instead.

Whatever the reason, too few players know how to bunt. That's a shame, because if you have good bat control and have average to above-average running speed, you can make bunting into a solid part of your game.

Look at Kenny Lofton of the Indians. He bunts at least once a game, and when he does, he puts great pressure on the opposing team. True, Kenny has tremendous speed and bats left-handed, but those two assets would mean nothing if he didn't know how to bunt.

Many coaches say that bunting is easy, that it's just a matter of getting the job done. Well, that's not right. Bunting is a skill that players must learn and practice, over and over. Today's best bunters, like Lofton and Omar Vizquel, work at their bunting day after day. Brett Butler might devote his entire batting practice to bunting just to get his timing down.

Let's start with bunting for a hit, because if you master that you should be able to execute a sacrifice bunt easily. Besides, most young players want to bunt for a hit.

The key here is to see the pitch, get your hands in bunting position, and make contact with the pitch. Only then should you start running. Too many young players start running to first before they make contact. As a result, they either miss the pitch, foul it off, or attempt to bunt a pitch that is clearly a ball. Yes, the element of surprise can make your bunt more effective. If you become good enough and quick enough with your hands to drop the bat into bunting position at the last second, then you have an advantage. That ability comes only from a great deal of practice. Frankly, most young hitters don't practice this craft enough.

Keep these points in mind when bunting for a hit:

1. Keep your arms extended and straight, but keep your hands soft. Soft hands will deaden the ball on the bat.

Keep your arms away from your body. If you hold them too close, you'll find yourself poking at the pitch.

2. Keep your arms level and parallel to the ground. If you start to dip with the bat, you'll foul off the pitch or pop it up.

3. You don't have to bunt the first pitch you see. The third baseman is always ready on the first pitch. Try putting down a bunt when the count is 2-0 or 2-1. That's when you'll find the third baseman napping.

4. The best kind of pitch to bunt is a low pitch or a breaking pitch. The hardest ones to bunt are fastballs, high and away. Remember, if you don't like the pitch, you don't have to bunt it.

5. The best bunts are usually down the third-base line, but you can also push a bunt toward the second baseman. It's a tough play for the second sacker to rush in, scoop up the ball, and fire back across his body to first.

Sacrifice Bunts

When you get the sign from your coach to put down a sacrifice bunt, you know that he's already decided that you're going to give up your at-bat for the good of the team. You may be disappointed, but you have to accept it. If you don't, then you'll make only a half-hearted attempt at a sacrifice, and you'll let down the team and your coach (and yourself).

So I tell my players that when they see the sacrifice sign, they should take a moment to let their personal disappointment pass. ("Darn, coach," all hitters say to themselves, "let me hit away! I don't want to bunt!") Then they must start focusing on the task at hand.

Sacrificing yourself means just that. Make certain you square around in plenty of time to get the bunt down. There's no deception involved here. Oddly enough, many players wait too long to square around to a bunting position. Remember— it's a sacrifice!

Once you do square around, you should be in perfect bunting position: arms fully extended, bat parallel to the ground, knees bent, and hands in bunting position. Remember, you should bunt only at strikes. A sacrifice bunt is not the same as a suicide squeeze bunt, when you have to bunt at the pitch and make contact.

Ideally, you should aim a sacrifice bunt away from the pitcher, toward either third or first. Again, this takes practice. It doesn't happen by itself.

For most bunters, whether bunting to sacrifice or bunting for a hit, the best approach is to aim at a target on the grass, perhaps a few feet down the line or somewhere on the grass a few feet from the plate. By focusing on where you want to bunt the ball, you seem to gain a better idea of how to execute the bunt and get the job done. Try it.

Slap Bunt

Players who really want to handle a bat should experiment with a slap bunt. Use this play when you and everyone in the ballpark knows that it's a bunt situation, when it's so obvious you will bunt that the infielders are charging in madly as you square around.

To make the slap bunt effective, remember that you're not trying to hit a home run. All you really want to do is hit the ball hard while the fielders are charging in. A hard-slapped ball will catch the fielders off balance. Ideally, you'll move the runners along and get on base as well.

To do this properly, you have to square around as the pitcher is in his stretch. That sets the trap. As the defensive players charge in, bring your bat back. Since you're choked up on the bat, all you want to do is punch at the pitch. If you hit the ball hard, ideally on the ground or a line drive, the element of surprise will catch the fielders off guard.

BASIC LAWS OF BASE RUNNING

While you may not be as fast as Kenny Lofton, you can still make a big difference on the bases.

Most base runners are too cautious. Even worse, they don't plan when they get on base. Just as you have to plan out what you're going to do at the plate, or what you're going to do if the ball is hit to you in the field, you need a plan when you get on base.

The first thing is to know how many outs there are. That's essential. You should know that you never try to steal third, for example, when there are two outs (because you can score just as easily from second as you can from third when there are two outs). Basic base-running strategies like this are usually explained by your coach, and all of them are based on common sense. Knowing how many outs there are is your first step to strategic base running.

YOUR BASE-RUNNING CHECKLIST

When you reach base, you should keep an eye on the following items:

- Does the pitcher have a good pickoff move? Does he use it?
- Is the pitcher breaking a lot of curves into the dirt in front of the plate?
- Does the catcher have a good arm?
- Is the backstop close to the catcher, or can I make it to the next base on a passed ball?
- Is the infield dirt soft or hard? Is it a fast track to run on?
- Who is the batter?
- What does the coach want me to do (in other words, what signs is he giving me)?

These thoughts should be racing through your head. Of course, you can answer many of the questions while watching from the bench. It's during those moments that you can check out the pitcher's pickoff moves and the catcher's arm. Work on your base-running strategies not only when you get on base but also at other times during the game.

You're too young to have ever seen the great Jackie Robinson run the bases for the Brooklyn Dodgers. Jackie was perhaps the best base runner of all time. Robinson was particularly gifted at faking and feinting when he took a lead off any base. As a result, the pitcher couldn't concentrate fully on the batter, the catcher had to worry about Jackie breaking for the next base, and the infielders had to cheat a little in their defensive stances to be closer to a base in case Jackie did steal.

The overall result was disaster for the defense. Because the defense couldn't focus exclusively on the batter, they ran into all sorts of problems. My advice? When you get on base, start working on your moves to keep the defense jittery. Believe me, it will work wonders for you—and the best part is that you don't even have to be that fast. The key is to make the opposing team aware of your presence on the bases.

Stealing

Again, the best base stealers are the ones who plan ahead. That means knowing how to get a good jump on the pitcher, and the only way you can do that is by studying the pitcher's pickoff move.

Baseball experts often point out that the fastest sprinter on the team often isn't the best base stealer. Raw speed alone isn't enough. You have to know how to read the pitcher. Again, that means studying him when your teammates are on base.

Most pitchers (both righty and lefty) develop a series of pickoff moves. They have a lazy one, then a better one, and then their best one. It's up to you to get him to show all three. If you're the first member of your team to reach first base, you should make the pitcher reveal his best moves to you and the rest of your team.

Once you've seen his best, you can pick up telltale signs of what he's going to do. Perhaps he does something with his head, or with his leg kick, or with the way he reaches back with the ball. When you learn how he tips off his move, you can anticipate what he's going to do with the ball.

Anticipation is the key to stealing. If you wait until you're absolutely certain that he's going home with the pitch, then your jump will be a poor one. If you anticipate correctly—and yes, this means taking a risk—then you have an excellent chance of stealing successfully. It means knowing the pitcher's habits and being willing to take a calculated gamble to steal.

What do you do if you guess wrong and are picked off? Simple. Just don't stop. Keep sprinting at top speed to second base and slide. By the time the first baseman gets the ball out of his glove and throws to second base, you might be safe. But if you stop running because you were picked off, you're always going to be a dead duck. So keep running hard.

Sliding

Sliding can be difficult for many young players. That's too bad because it can be an effective part of your baseball repertoire. Whether you prefer to hook slide, fade, or slide headfirst, you have to practice it.

When I coached sliding, I usually waited for a rainy day when the outfield grass was soft and wet. I had the players remove their shoes (important!) and slide on the wet grass. This gave them confidence that they wouldn't get strawberries or bruises on their legs. Furthermore, they could practice proper technique without fear of twisting their ankles.

With a conventional feet-first slide, make certain to keep your hands high in the air behind you. By doing this you land more on your buttocks than your knees, which is essential for protecting yourself. This also keeps your feet in the air so that you can't sprain an ankle.

Some players grip batting gloves or handfuls of dirt to keep their hands from being bruised on the ground; that's a good idea too. Remember, the idea is to land on your butt and thighs, not scrape along on your shins and knees.

Above all, once you start to slide, don't stop. The majority of injuries occur when a player starts to slide but then decides to stop halfway, either because he realizes he doesn't have to or because the fielder tells him not to. That's when you get hurt.

MAKING THE INNING BIG

The one vital ingredient for playing your best offensive baseball is courage. You can't play this game passively. To reach your maximum offensive potential, you must persuade yourself to take chances. Try to put down a bunt for a hit, try to take a longer lead, try to take that extra base, and so on.

This all may sound silly, but the truth is that most players get to a point in their career where they aren't as aggressive and courageous as they once were. Players can be overcome by the fear that they will make an out. When you start worrying about making outs and begin to play offense cautiously, it's time to realize that you're going down the wrong path.

Step your game up to a higher level. Be aggressive. Take a chance. Play the game with the kind of confidence that you have always shown in the past. Ultimately, that's the key to better baseball—and better yet, that's something you can control.

6

BECOMING A TOP-FLIGHT DEFENSIVE PLAYER

Just about every lecture ever given on playing defense starts with this suggestion: "Know what you're going to do with the ball before it's hit to you."

Certainly it's good advice. It must be—every coach who has ever hit a fungo agrees with it. But what does it actually mean? More important, how do you put this age-old advice into action?

In its simplest terms, the admonition means that no matter what position you play in the field, you have to determine *before each pitch* the following items:

- How many outs are there?
- What's the score?
- What inning is it?
- Who's on base?
- What are the field conditions (sun, wind, rain, tall grass, hard-baked infield, and so forth)?
- Who do I throw the ball to if it comes to me (do I throw to first, to home, or to the cutoff man)?
- Should I play shallow or deep?
- If the ball is hit slowly at me, where do I make the play?
- Likewise, if the ball is hit sharply at me, what do I do with it?

Welcome to the mental chess game of baseball. Ironically, the more baseball you play, the more complicated it becomes. Somebody once said that baseball was a relatively simple game. I think whoever said that didn't truly understand the nature of the sport, because baseball gets more complicated as you go up the ladder of competition.

Countless questions should be whirring through your mind as you get set for every pitch. You have to go through this mental gymnastic before every pitch, perhaps a hundred or more times each game. That involves concentration, concentration, and more concentration.

Of course, many defensive situations are routine. For example, your team is leading 6-0, and it's the eighth inning. You're playing right field, and with nobody on and two out, a batter hits a routine fly to you. All you have to do is catch the ball, and the side is retired. You need not worry here about runners tagging up or about hitting the cutoff man.

OK, that's easy. But what about this defensive situation? The game is tied 2-2 in the eighth inning. There's one out, and the other team has a man on third. You're playing second base. You note that the runner on third has pretty good speed. The batter is right-handed. He hits a three-hopper that scoots past the pitcher on its way up the middle. You sprint over in front of second and cut it off.

Do you throw home to try to get the runner? Or do you give up the run and throw the batter out at first? You've also noted that the grass is damp and fairly high.

If you haven't thought about this situation *before* it happens, then your chances of executing the right defensive play are very slim. That's what baseball coaches mean when they say you have to know what you're going to do with the ball before it's hit to you. (By the way, chances are that you ought to throw the runner out at first because a runner with good speed is going to score once he sees the ground ball go past the pitcher, especially when the infield grass is tall and wet, making it difficult to handle the ball.)

In my experience, I find that coaches and managers always complain that young professional baseball players just don't play enough baseball to have mastered the instincts of the game. Now, instincts are somewhat difficult to define, but it's the idea that you automatically know what to do on a baseball field without having to be told or instructed. As a fielder, that means knowing when to back up a base in case of an errant throw. It means automatically knowing when to pick off a runner. It means knowing when to hold the ball rather than risking a throw that might be a poor one.

The combination of knowing what to do if the ball is hit to you plus having an instinct for the game should insure that you're ready defensively. Knowing what to do on each play is something you can learn and study; developing instincts, however, only comes from playing enough baseball that you see and understand the various situations that can occur in a game.

MENTAL SKILLS FOR DEFENSE

How do you get better at sharpening your mind for defense? Easy. Just get in the habit of being observant when you watch or play the game. No matter what position you play, start looking around. Observe and then ask yourself questions, as in these examples:

1. This batter is a big power hitter. Should I think about playing deeper?
2. Our pitcher is not throwing hard anymore. Should I start playing this batter to pull the ball?
3. But I see the catcher is trying to set up his target on the outside of the plate. That means the pitcher is going to try to pitch this guy away.
4. The batter has pulled rockets to the third baseman all day. I'd better play a little deeper. I can probably get away with it because while the batter is big, he's also very slow.

You get the idea. As Hall of Famer Yogi Berra once said, "You can see a lot by just watching." Truer words were never spoken about baseball.

The trick is to develop the mental discipline to do this on every pitch. Infielders and catchers usually come to this discipline rather quickly because there's so much action in the infield. Outfielders must learn not to stew about their batting average and their swing, and pay more attention to who is batting and where to play them.

I remember playing in a particularly tight game and coming off after the final out with a severe headache. I was exhausted from the mental gymnastics of preparing myself on every pitch in case the ball was hit to me. As it developed, I didn't physically handle a ball all day. I recall my teammate asking me why I was so tired since I hadn't handled the ball. It was the mental chess game that had worn me out. Thinking is hard work, and not knowing what's going to happen but having to prepare for it is perhaps the most difficult work.

One last word on mental preparation. Must you have a genius IQ to be a star ballplayer? Of course not. But any major leaguer will tell you how complex this game is. True, not every major leaguer can discuss Einstein's theory of relativity, but they can sure tell you what it means to prepare mentally for each play in a game.

DEFENSIVE PLAY IN THE INFIELD

If you play the infield (and this includes pitchers, because once you've thrown a pitch to the batter, you're an infielder), you should start off with a medium-sized glove, well broken in, with a full sewn-in web. Gloves that are too large or too stiff will make your plays more difficult. Make certain the stitching in the fingers is tight and that the web is closed so that balls can't get lodged there and become difficult to remove.

Your Defensive Position

Besides preparing yourself mentally, you must also get in the habit of preparing yourself physically for every pitch. Playing infield is a matter of quickness, of starts and stops in various directions. Just as you get ready to break when you take a lead to steal a base, you have to be ready to move when you're playing defense.

Take a look at how pro tennis players wait for a serve. You'll notice that they bounce around on their toes, moving a bit, ready to spring to action. The best infielders use the same mechanism. Get in the habit of bending your knees, stay on the balls of your feet, and always assume that the next ball is going to be drilled right at you.

That's the best way to wake yourself up and keep yourself ready for action. Over the course of a game in which more than one hundred pitches are thrown, you're going to find yourself becoming mentally fatigued, especially if your pitchers are going deep into the count with every batter. But sure enough, just when you let your guard down, the ball is going to be hit right at you.

Improve Your Range

Many infielders think that range is a function only of foot speed. Actually, range is a function of quickness, foot speed, anticipation, and most important, placement in the field. Great plays in the field usually start with where the infielder placed himself *before* he made the play. When an infielder flags down a ball far to one side or the other, people in the stands marvel at his range only because they didn't know where he was positioned before the pitch. That's why it's so important to determine where you should position yourself, depending on the batter, the pitcher, the game situation, and so on.

One of the best ways to improve your range is to improve your reaction time. Try the following drill. Go out to shortstop and turn around to face the outfield. Get in your ready defensive position. Have your coach stand near the pitching mound and gently fungo ground balls to your left or right. At the crack of the bat, you have to turn, find the ball, and make the play.

I saw Brian Graham, one of the top up-and-coming managerial prospects in pro ball, use this drill extensively in spring training, during the regular season, and during the fall instructional league with all his infield prospects. It was extraordinary to see how it helped these players learn to stay on their toes and react quickly to the ball. Players improved their range tremendously in both directions. This drill emphasizes your readiness on every play, decreases your reaction time, and forces you to make the play quickly.

One last note on range for shortstops and second basemen. On a ball hit up the middle, your best bet is to take a quick look at the ball and then sprint to where you think the ball is going to be and where you can reach it. By not watching the ball the entire way, you can run and move faster. Take a quick look, run to the anticipated spot, and find the ball with your eyes again. By doing this you can add two feet to your range in either direction.

Develop Soft Hands

Scouts always talk about an infielder having soft hands. While this attribute is somewhat innate, you can improve your

a

b

Stand with your back to the batter (a). Turn at the crack of the bat and find the ball (b).

flexibility when it comes to fielding and catching a ball by doing a simple exercise.

Lie down on your bed (say at night, before you get ready for sleep) and practice catching a tennis ball with arms extended. Catch the ball with both hands and then quickly flip it back into the air. It's an easy drill at first, but after you've done 50 or 60 consecutive catch and throws, you'll find that your arms become tired and your hands get a bit stiff and achy. That's the precise time to concentrate even more on the catch and flip.

This is not only a great way to soften your hands (after all, you can't catch a tennis ball with "hard" hands), it's also good technique for middle infielders who want to become more accustomed to handling a ball while making a pivot.

Another time-tested method of developing soft hands is using the wooden glove in infield work. Rather than using your regular leather fielding glove, you slip on a wooden glove that forces you to catch the ball gently with both hands. Obviously, if your hands aren't soft, the ground ball will simply ricochet off the glove.

The wooden-glove drill forces you to "give" with the ball as you field. That makes your hands, wrists, and arms more pliable, so that there is a more graceful rhythm in your fielding. Many high school, college, and pro players use the wooden glove as part of their preseason routine.

Learn to Communicate

An essential part of playing defense is knowing how to communicate with your teammates. No position on the field is suitable for shy ballplayers. In the infield, you should maintain a constant stream of meaningful chatter with your teammates. Talk about how many outs there are, what this batter did last time, how the pitcher is pitching his game. And, of course, discuss who's covering second base on a steal attempt, on a delayed steal, and on and on.

When a man is on first at higher levels of ball, the second baseman and shortstop before each pitch communicate through hidden face signals which of them is covering second on an attempted steal. The idea is that when the middle infielders see the catcher's sign and recognize whether the next pitch is going to be an off-speed pitch (which is easily pulled by the batter) or a fast ball (which is not normally pulled), then the shortstop can decide who's going to cover second base.

For example, suppose a right-handed batter is facing a righty pitcher. The shortstop sees the catcher give the sign for a curveball. He motions to the second baseman by opening his mouth. That means that the shortstop, expecting the curveball to be pulled and hit to him, wants the second baseman to cover the steal. Likewise, if it's a fastball, the shortstop will keep his mouth closed to the second baseman, indicating that the shortstop will cover second base. Note that the middle infielders shield their signals by using their gloves to cover their facial actions. The shortstop and second baseman do this on every pitch in pro ball when there's a man on first base. Watch for it the next time you go to a pro game.

Other communication includes constantly reminding your outfielders of the number of outs, communicating with your teammates on cutoffs and relays, and of course, being your teammates' extra eyes when their backs are to a play.

How to Make the Pivot if You're a Second Baseman

The pivot has been described as a fancy dance step. Well, that's true to a certain extent, because obviously your feet are involved. But there's also a throw to handle, and that can make your work around the bag a little more complicated.

I've found over the years that the best way to explain the pivot is to break it down into various parts and then build from there.

Move to Double-Play Depth

First, when you're playing second, you must learn how to position yourself at double-play depth. The position you take is dictated by the requirement that you be at the bag waiting for the throw before it gets there. If you arrive just as the ball is getting there, you're too late. There's nothing worse than seeing a double play scotched because the pivot man got there too late.

To protect against this happening, you must cheat a little toward the bag when you're at double-play depth. That doesn't mean you have to stand right next to the bag before the pitch

Be at the bag before the ball is thrown.

is thrown, but take a chance and move a little closer to second than you normally would. In infield practice, you can calculate just how quickly you can get to second base to receive a throw from a fellow infielder. Once you know how quickly you can get there, start making those accommodations in a game. Just make certain you get to second base and are waiting for that throw.

Assume a Bad Throw

You have to be at the bag before the throw gets there because you may get a poor feed from the other infielder. By getting to the bag early, you can prepare yourself for a bad feed (when, for example, the throw is low, high, wide, or off the mark entirely).

By expecting a bad throw, you can bend your knees a bit, get your hands extended from your body, and then make any final movement to receive the poor throw. Above all, get at least one out on the play. That may mean you just catch the poor feed throw and don't even try for the second out. That's OK as long as you get that first one.

Don't Straddle the Bag

When moving in and around second base for a pivot, don't plant your feet on either side or, for that matter, stand next to the bag in the base line between first and second. If you do, you're putting yourself in the way of the base runner who's sliding hard into second. That makes you an easy, and vulnerable, target. Instead, try to stand either off to one side of the bag or even right behind it. Give the base line to the runner; you'll take everything else.

Keep Your Hand Extended, Open, and Even

Keep your glove around your midsection, open and ready to catch the feed throw. Catch the ball with *both* hands. If you catch the ball with your glove and then have to reach into it to pull the ball out and throw it, you'll lose the split second you may need to complete the play.

Try to catch the ball while pulling it out to throw in the same quick motion. One trick is to take the middle finger of your left hand (your glove hand) and, while it's in the glove, push it against the pocket of your glove. When you catch the ball, the middle finger acts like an internal spring that quickly pushes the ball into your throwing hand. Try it a few times. It will make the transition from caught ball to thrown ball smooth and quick.

Dance Around the Base

Most of the time you will get a good feed when you're making a pivot. To make a simple but solid throw to first, position yourself right behind the bag, toward the right-field side. When the throw comes in, catch it, and then merely touch the tip of the base with your left foot. Do not step over the base.

After brushing the bag with your left toe, simply rock your weight onto your back foot and then aim your left foot toward first. This quick two-step motion allows you to touch the bag and then push off your back foot to get a solid throw to first. Even better, because you'll never be in the base line, there's little chance of being hit by the sliding base runner.

If the throw is on the pitcher's mound side of the bag (that is, between the grass side of the infield and second base), then you will have to come across the bag to catch the ball and make

a

b

Catch the ball with both hands (a) and tag with both (b).

the throw. Here, you start from the same position, but you step on second base with your left foot and land on your right foot inside the bag. You then make your throw to first off the right foot. Even though you're now on the inside part of the infield, you can still make a solid throw to first (off your back foot) and you're out of the base path.

Make a Solid Throw

Because you'll be making your pivot throws off your back foot (your right foot), you should be able to get some real zip on your throw to first. Too many second basemen get their feet tangled up and end up making a soft lob to first. The beauty of this system is that you know you'll get off a good throw.

Don't worry about the base runner. Remember, he's sliding toward the base, not toward you. Besides, you're not in the base path. You should be throwing either from the outfield side of the base or from the inside of the infield.

a   b

Quick two-step motion gets the ball to first faster. Touch the bag with your left foot (a), rock back (b) and throw.

Remember that there are many moving parts here. Have a teammate throw you easy feeds from only a few feet away as you learn the various aspects of making a pivot. Once you feel a natural rhythm developing, you can start working on taking, and making, longer throws around the pivot.

DEFENSIVE PLAY IN THE OUTFIELD

Playing the outfield involves several skills that are sometimes not obvious to younger players. For example, excellent foot speed is, of course, important for all outfielders. But just as important as foot speed is getting a good jump on the ball. The same goes for a strong and accurate arm; that's important, but so is having a quick release on throws. Playing the outfield isn't as easy as it may seem.

Know How to Position Yourself

Keep the following points in mind when positioning yourself in the outfield:

1. Who is pitching for your team? Does he throw hard? Or is he mostly a change-of-speed artist? Naturally, you'll want to favor one way or the other in the outfield, depending on whether you think the other team is going to pull the ball or be late in their swings.

2. What is the wind doing today? Is it calm? Is the breeze steady or gusty? Never take the wind for granted. The breeze affects the flight of fly balls, particularly high fly balls. Check the wind's direction before each inning by tossing a few blades of grass in the air.

3. What is the grass like in the outfield? Is it tall? Does it need to be cut? Or is the outfield hard-baked and thin on grass? Is it bumpy? Knowing these conditions will help you determine how to position yourself. On a hard-baked, asphaltlike outfield, you'll have to play deep to prevent singles from becoming triples as the ball gains momentum. On the other hand, if the grass is tall, you'll have to charge every ball that's hit to you.

   On a bumpy outfield, you can never assume that the ball will quietly roll to you where you can merely scoop it up with your glove. You will probably have to get down on one knee for every ball to block it if it happens to take a bad hop. Always remind yourself and your outfield buddies to get down on every ball hit to the outfield.

4. Who is the batter? Does it look like he has power? Or is he a slap hitter? What did he do on his last at-bat?

The more you play against an opponent, the easier it becomes to play defense against them because you learn their abilities, strengths, and habits at the plate.

Position yourself in the outfield by considering these key points. Just remember that playing the outfield is more than just running out to the same spot inning after inning. The best defensive plays in the outfield start by positioning yourself in the right spot before the pitch is thrown.

Getting in Ready Position

To play the outfield well, you must get a jump on the ball on every pitch. Doing so is probably even more important in the outfield than it is in the infield. To "get a jump" on the ball you must be so focused on the pitch and swing that you find yourself moving toward where the ball is going to be hit even before the batter makes contact.

It takes a little experience to develop this ability, but if you have ever played center field for even a few innings, you probably found yourself moving and swaying on every pitch. That moving and swaying is the origin of getting a jump.

Make certain you have your knees bent and that you're on the balls of your feet just as the pitch is being released. Keep your hand and gloved hand off your knees and be ready to move in any direction. When you find your body moving on every pitch, learn to trust your instincts. Don't fight them. If you find yourself moving to either the left or the right, go with it.

Some outfielders are particularly good at going back on the ball. Others are much more comfortable coming in on a fly. Determine what you do better and adjust your position in the outfield accordingly. If you aren't sure what you're better at, simply ask your coach. He'll know.

The most difficult play you'll have to make as an outfielder is the line drive hit right at you. For a brief moment, your eyes have difficulty perceiving the path of a ball hit with velocity directly to you. Once you learn to develop and trust your fielding instincts, you'll be fine. Have your coach hit line drives at you in practice to develop this skill.

Practice Cutoffs and Relays

Like the infielders, you have to know where you're throwing the ball *before* each pitch is thrown. This is vitally important in the outfield because you are the last line of defense. In a close game, throwing the ball to the wrong base or missing the cutoff man can cost your team the game.

For example, in a game that your team is winning 3-2 in the eighth inning, the other team has a man on second with one out. You're playing center field. You have a good, but not great, arm. The man on second has excellent speed. The next batter hits a ground-ball base hit up the middle. You field it cleanly, and you're sorely tempted to try to throw the runner out at home.

But remember this. If you try to throw out a speedy runner on a ground ball up the middle, chances are that you won't even be close. He'll tie the game at 3-3, and the batter, who normally would have stopped at first base, will now have a chance to go on to second base and put himself in scoring position for the next batter. You're better off conceding the run so that you can keep the batter at first where he's not in a position to score and win the game on another base hit.

I once saw a left fielder in pro ball drop a long foul ball on purpose because the winning run was on third base and the runner would have scored easily by tagging up after the catch. The left fielder realized that even though he could have caught the ball, it made better sense to let it drop and take a chance on the next pitch retiring the batter. That's the kind of thinking before the play that goes into playing the outfield.

One last note on cutoffs and relays. If you concentrate on what you're doing, you should never miss hitting a cutoff man. Throw the ball straight, accurately, and on a line, and you'll do fine. This only takes concentration.

Here's a simple and fun drill you can do on your own to improve your throws from the outfield. Take a large, empty trash bin and about a dozen baseballs to the field. Place the bin on its side next to the pitcher's mound, with the open mouth facing the outfield. Take your baseballs to the outfield and place them on the ground. Back up about 20 feet and then run at a ball as though it were a base hit. Scoop it up and fire a strike to the bin. Try to hit the bin on a line.

After doing this drill, place the bin on home plate. Do the same drill as before except this time try to throw the ball on one

a

b

Improve your accuracy on cutoffs and relays. Place a trash can on home plate. Practice hitting the cutoff and relay (a-b).

hop into the open bin. These drills will improve not only your arm strength but also your accuracy on cutoff throws.

Use Four-Seam Throws

Just about every throw from the outfield should be a four-seam throw. Also, you should always throw overhand, never sidearm. A throw that comes in from an outfielder to the plate or to the cutoff man is infinitely easier to handle if it takes a true, straight hop. If you throw a ball sidearm or three-quarters, the throw will skitter and take an awkward hop when it hits the ground.

Throwing with your fingers cutting across all four seams of the ball will give it that straight, true hop, especially if you have mastered the art of throwing the ball totally over the top. Such a motion, by the way, will also increase your distance and velocity. The best time to practice this method is during infield/outfield practice before the game.

Balls from the outfield should always be thrown overhand, using all four seams.

Back Up Your Teammates

Often overlooked until a ball gets by your teammate in a game, backing up your fellow outfielders is a major part of defensive play. Being a last line of defense is especially important when you play on bumpy or rock-hard outfields.

This demands extreme hustle on your part. Most of the time, of course, the ball won't get through. But when the ball does get by, you'll impress your coach, your teammates, yourself (and the scouts) by being in the right place at the right time. It's just good baseball.

Communicate With Your Teammates

Again, like infielders, outfielders must communicate. You have to direct traffic for your teammate as he's catching a fly ball, telling him where he's going to throw it or reminding him how many outs there are. Likewise, you want him to provide similar instructions as you field a fly or ground ball. You can't concentrate on making the catch if you're trying to figure out where to throw the ball.

Of course it's essential that you and your colleagues communicate well on every fly ball that comes into your shared territory. Outfielders must listen for their teammate's voice when both of them are chasing a fly ball or pop-up. Otherwise, a dangerous collision can occur.

Keep the basics in mind—a center fielder gets priority on every fly ball. If he calls for the play, then the right and left fielders must back off. When you do call to make the catch, don't be bashful. Yell it out so not only do your outfield colleagues hear you but the infielders hear you too.

Get Through the Boredom

The biggest mental obstacle for most outfielders is coping with the extensive downtime. You might play an entire game and not once get a fly ball or ground ball. That, as you well know, can quickly become boring.

Many outfielders use this extra time in the outfield to think about their batting strokes. You'll even see outfielders swinging an invisible bat in the outfield between pitches. That's a pretty good tip-off to any coach that a player is thinking about his offense when he's supposed to be thinking about his defense.

Look upon the downtime in the outfield as a kind of mental challenge. The beauty, and the frustration, of baseball is that you never know when a ball might be hit to you. Consequently, you should be priming yourself on every pitch. When the ball is finally hit to you, you'll know that you're fully prepared to make the play.

Divide the game into series of three outs. When you take the field for each inning, mentally remind yourself to be prepared for each out of just that inning. Who knows? Three line drives might be hit at you that inning, and that's what you should be thinking about as you get ready for each pitch. The other team gets only 27 outs a game. If you have a chance to make any of those putouts, you want to be ready. At the end of each half-inning, just put it behind you, and look forward to the next half-inning when you're back out in the field.

Believe it or not, this simple kind of acute mental concentration will propel you into becoming the best outfielder you can be. It means that you'll always be sharp, ready to get a good jump on the ball, and know what to do with the ball if you field it. Regardless of your physical attributes, if you're always in a set position, ready to go, then you'll always be on top of the play.

DEFENSIVE PLAY AS A CATCHER

Being a successful catcher involves much more than just calling and catching pitches. Every scout will tell you that the catcher is the first defensive player he focuses on, that the catcher should be the natural leader on the field.

That doesn't mean that the catcher must be the loudest player on the field (although that doesn't hurt), or that the catcher must be largest player (although that wouldn't hurt either). What it does mean is that the catcher must develop an on-field personality like that of a field general—a field general who directs his defensive troops for every batter, who reminds everybody how many outs there are, who directs the cutoffs and relays, who keeps the infielders and outfielders on their toes, who hustles down to first to back up every infield throw.

Of course, the catcher must also have the ability to receive every pitch and throw out would-be base stealers.

It's a broad job description, to say the least. But the more catching you do, and the more big-league catchers you watch, the more all of this will become second nature to you. For example, some younger catchers are understandably reserved behind the plate. After all, if the catcher is a sophomore in school, who is he to direct the infielders and outfielders if most of them are juniors and seniors?

Take Command of the Field

That's part of the catcher's job. Even if you have to force yourself into that role, that's the job you've undertaken. It's called taking command behind the plate. All the best catchers do it. When the catcher is full of pep and energy, then the entire team follows suit. They just automatically lift up their game to match the energy level of the catcher.

Scouts, coaches, teammates, and pitchers love an energetic catcher. He brings an extra zest to the game and reassures his teammates that he is fully in command.

The Cleveland Indians had a very talented catching prospect a few years ago. This catcher had all the tools—he could hit, throw, and run—but he lacked one thing, a presence behind the plate. Even though he was a good-sized catcher, he was a quiet young man. He didn't make any noise behind the plate and rarely took command of the game.

The Indians worked long and hard to help him develop a stronger personality. They made him work in the bullpen specifically on evolving his personality into an outgoing and dominant one. Alas, it didn't work—he just felt uncomfortable being a field general behind the plate.

What did the Indians do with him? They traded him. After all, he still had all the physical skills. He just didn't have enough of a presence to dominate their big-league club, the way catchers like Sandy Alomar Jr. or Tony Pena do.

If you think that you're a bit too bashful behind the plate, try working on your leadership style and presence in front of a mirror at home. That's right—practice what you yell out, practice what you look like, practice how you take command of the team. This exercise may seem a bit goofy at first, but the more you project yourself as the leader of the team on the field, the sooner you'll feel more comfortable with your new approach.

Check Your Equipment

Some catchers always keep a checklist with them to make certain they don't forget anything when they pack their bag to go to the ballpark. If you've ever had that sinking feeling of realizing you left your mitt or face mask at home on the kitchen counter, then you know what a good idea it is to have a checklist.

Other ballplayers need only to remember to bring a bat and glove, but as a catcher you've got to load up the entire store before you head out for the game. As a result, it's easy to forget something.

Beyond that, you should constantly check your equipment during the year for wear and tear. Make certain all the straps are tight and strong. Make sure your equipment is well marked with your name so that you never lose it.

You should break in your catcher's glove thoroughly before you use it in a game. Most big-league catchers carry at least two mitts: one's their gamer, and the other is their backup in case they tear a strap on their game mitt during a game. In addition there's usually a third catcher's mitt somewhere in their bag that they're breaking in when they're catching in the bullpen.

Now, most young catchers can't afford to have more than one mitt at a time. That's OK, but that's why it's doubly important to make certain that your mitt is in fine working order before each game. Checking the straps for wear and tear is essential; after all, if your glove snaps a string in the fourth inning and you don't have a backup ready, then you'll have to borrow somebody else's catcher's glove to finish the game. As you know, that can cause all sorts of problems when trying to catch a hard-throwing pitcher.

Call Pitches

On the mental side of baseball, as you go up the ladder, how each opposing batter is pitched becomes exceedingly important. At the junior high level, of course, if your pitcher throws hard and throws strikes, then it's just a matter of squatting down and giving him a good target. As you get into high school, college, and pro ball, however, calling a good game becomes the mark of an outstanding catcher. Now, much of this ability simply comes from baseball experience, but you're never too young to start thinking about how to pitch to a batter.

Just as the infielders and outfielders examine the batter's size, speed, power, and so forth, you, as the catcher, should do the same. Because of your proximity to the batter in the batter's box, you have the best observation point to check on just how far (or how close) he stands from the plate, how heavy (or how small) his bat is, whether he's got an open or closed stance, whether he looks like he wants to bunt, and so on.

With your knowledge of what your pitcher is throwing well that day (fastball, curve, slider, change, and so forth), your knowledge of how the umpire is calling balls and strikes (giving you the corners, or perhaps the low strike, or maybe the high strike), and your instinctive knowledge of hitters, you can begin to plot out a game plan on how to set up each hitter.

In general, you want your pitcher to get ahead of the batter. In the amateur divisions it's rare to see a batter swing at the first pitch he sees, so it's often a good idea to have your pitcher throw a fastball for strike one. Even if that pattern becomes apparent to your opponents, you'll still find it infrequent for the amateur batter to swing at the first pitch.

Once you get that first pitch over for a strike, the advantage goes right away to the pitcher. Now, in preparation for the second pitch, you and the pitcher can experiment a bit. Should you throw the curve? The change? The fastball again? The batter, once he's behind in the count, is more defensive at the plate and more likely to chase a bad pitch.

This, of course, is the essence of the pitcher-batter matchup. As the catcher, you're the one who orchestrates all this. When you see that a batter is crowding the plate, you have to make your pitcher back him off by pitching him inside. If another batter has a problem hitting the curveball, keep that in the back of your mind so that you can call for the curve whenever you want to finish off that batter.

If the ninth batter in the lineup is up and he stands far from the plate, there's no reason for your pitcher to labor too hard. Have him throw fastball strikes until the hitter proves that he can get around on the pitch and make sharp contact. Should you throw a change-up to the number-nine batter? Well, by doing that, you're doing him a favor. The reason he's batting ninth is because he's probably not as gifted a hitter as his teammates. By throwing him an off-speed pitch, you're giving him a better chance to be successful.

A BRIEF RECAP ON CALLING PITCHES

Get in the habit of checking these points in your mind as you plot your strategy for each batter:

1. How is my pitcher throwing? Is his fastball sharp today? Can he control his curve? Is he throwing strikes? Is he getting ahead of the batters? Is he tiring (losing velocity)?

2. Who is the batter? Does he have speed? Does he pull the ball? Does he slap it to all fields? Is he crowding the plate? Can we jam him? Will he try to bunt for a hit? Does he take many pitches?

3. What about the umpire? Is he calling a large or small strike zone? What about the corners? What about the low strike?

You often see pro pitchers and catchers talking on the mound throughout the game, or in the dugout between innings. They're discussing who's coming up next and how to pitch to him. Or whether the ump is giving them the low-and-away corner for a strike. Or whether the next batter is dying to hit a fastball, and if he is, they're deciding to throw him only off-speed stuff.

When you get to the point where you have these kinds of discussions with your pitcher, then you know you're on the right track as the team's field general—and, in many ways, as the brains behind the team's effort.

One last note: On many teams, both high school and college, the head coach will call the pitches from the dugout by using signs to the catcher. My personal feeling is that while it's OK for a coach to use signs with a catcher in a singular tight situation, a catcher is never going to learn how to call a game if he's always getting signs from the bench.

If you find yourself in this situation, ask your coach if you can occasionally have the freedom to call your own game. If he's reluctant, perhaps he will at least allow you to call games when the score is lopsided. That's a good compromise that will give you the chance to start working on your catching instincts.

Throw to Second and Third

As with everything else in baseball, learning the proper way to throw out runners is a matter of proper mechanical skills and strength. The more you practice this part of your game, the better you'll become. But you have to remember to keep practicing the right skills.

Think about quickness and arm strength. Those are the keys to a solid, accurate throw. Here are some helpful hints to improve your throwing game:

1. Practice your form in front of a mirror. I've suggested several times in this book that you use a mirror to see your form, and this is another good time to do so. Without using a ball, practice just your catching motion, footwork, and throw to second base.

    The sooner you learn to catch the ball, get in throwing position, and release the ball in short, quick form, the better off you'll be. It can be tricky, especially when you're catching a curveball that lands in the dirt, but you must master this throwing motion so that it becomes second nature to you.

2. When you practice your throws, throw to a spot in center field. To strengthen your arm, have your second baseman stand about 20 feet behind the bag and throw to him there. That way, when you have to throw to second base in a game, the throw will seem shorter. Of course, all throws should be straight, true, and level.

3. Throw over the top. Over the years a few catchers, most notably the late Yankees catcher Thurman Munson,

threw sidearm to second. While you might get a quicker release, the ball tends to sidewind into the runner coming down from first to second. It is extremely difficult for the infielder to catch the throw, especially if the throw is even a little bit off target. Throws over the top are straighter, more accurate, and easier for the infielder to handle.

4. To strengthen your throwing arm, do what the outfielders do—go out and practice long throws, from right field to left field. The more long throws you make, the stronger your arm will become. I recommend that you make this exercise a regular part of your daily workout. It will work wonders for your arm strength over the course of a season.

ONE LAST WORD

One of the best aspects of baseball is that it involves so many different skills. While many fans like to think about great slugging or great pitching, playing outstanding defense and making spectacular plays can often be more exciting and fulfilling than any other part of the game.

7

PITCHING—NOT THROWING—TO WIN

If you're a pitcher, you must start with the basics—determining what kind of pitcher you are.

Specifically, are you blessed with a great arm that can throw a ball with tremendous velocity, like Roger Clemens or John Smoltz? Or are you more of a control specialist, someone who can throw strikes all day, like Tom Glavine or Mark Clark? Perhaps you're a master at throwing off-speed pitches, including curves and changes that keep the batters off stride, like Jimmy Key or Dennis Martinez. Or maybe you're dreaming of becoming the next Tim Wakefield—a former minor-league first baseman who converted himself into a successful major-league knuckleball pitcher.

Most young pitchers assume that the only way they can win is to throw with impressive speed. Indeed, that may be true in the Little League divisions. Everybody has played on Little League teams where the biggest kid was the pitcher, simply because he could throw the hardest. Because he could throw so hard, he was usually tough to bat against because he was so wild and scary. But those days are pretty much over for you. As you progress into high school, college, and pro ball, pitching becomes an art form.

Want evidence? The most successful pitcher in the game today, and over the last decade, is Greg Maddux of the Atlanta Braves. Now, Greg features pitches with great control and great movement. Does he throw hard? Not particularly. Is he a big, threatening guy on the mound? Not at all. Greg is just an average-sized pitcher with just about average major-league velocity (82 to 85 miles per hour). But Greg has learned over the years that the key to successful pitching is to be consistent, to have a strategy for each batter, and to be able to hit certain locations.

In contrast, the guys who do throw hard—the guys who just go out on the mound, rear back, and fire—are usually effective for only a few years. When their velocity begins to decrease, they find that they have to make serious adjustments in their pitching style or they'll fall by the wayside. At the top echelons of baseball, all good hitters can hit a fastball, no matter how hard it's thrown. Even the great Nolan Ryan, whose fastball was clocked at upwards of 100 miles per hour, had a lifetime won-lost record of only around .500.

PITCHER'S BLUEPRINT FOR SUCCESS

Wouldn't it be helpful, then, to start to map out those ingredients for success—to aim for the kind of pitching mastery that Greg Maddux has?

To get you thinking along those lines, here's a quick outline of the physical and mental qualities that you should strive to develop. The great pitchers in baseball have all, or at least most, of these capabilities. If you aim for these qualities, you'll be on the right track:

1. Ability to throw a fastball with at least average major-league velocity (85 miles per hour)
2. Pinpoint control of the fastball
3. Total command of all your breaking pitches
4. Ability to change pitch speeds at any time
5. Capability to stay ahead in the count
6. Capacity to remember how each batter fared against you in the past
7. Savvy to make subtle adjustments to mechanics during the course of a game in case you run into trouble
8. Overall mental toughness to finish what you start
9. Consistent performance, game after game

If you possessed all these traits, you'd be right up with there with Greg Maddux. Chances are, though, that you haven't developed all these skills yet. That's OK. Don't be discouraged by looking at this blueprint; use it as a positive checklist—as a precise program of what you want to accomplish whenever you go to the mound, either in practice, in the bullpen, or in a game.

PREPARE TO THROW STRIKES

Let's start with the most important aspect of pitching—throwing strikes. If you can't throw the ball over the plate consistently, then you're not a pitcher—you're a thrower. Ask any of your teammates; if you can't throw strikes, you'll hurt your team more than you'll help it.

Many young pitchers complain that they have difficulty throwing strikes. Here's some good news. While you may not be able to improve your velocity much through practice, you can improve your control tremendously. All it takes is practice.

And here's more good news. All that practice time has an impact on your career for a long time. Once you get the hang of throwing strikes, your ability to do that stays with you. Most pitchers improve their control over the course of their careers, and it lasts through many pitching performances.

You can improve your control by doing any number of exercises, but all these drills have one thing in common—you have to keep doing them. Why more practice? Mounting scientific and medical evidence indicates that when you go through constant, repetitive motions with your arm, shoulders, fingers, and other interrelated nerves and muscles, you are really training the part of your brain that controls those voluntary motions.

Certain neuromuscular patterns, it's been theorized, can eventually become second nature, or automatic, for you if you practice those drills and skills long enough. For example, your pitching coach may ask you to try something a little different on the mound, maybe a new motion or a new way of holding the ball or some other little wrinkle. At first, the new way seems strange, foreign, even uncomfortable for you. You feel awkward, not at all smooth.

That feeling of awkwardness comes from the reality that your body has already developed a certain neuromuscular pattern that, over the passage of time, has come to feel natural and normal. Once you start changing, modifying, or challenging that comfortable style, your body sends a message that something feels goofy or strange.

Can these old, comfortable, and familiar neuromuscular patterns be changed for the better? You bet. True, it may take a few days, even weeks, of practice to get on the right track, but the sooner you start to reprogram and retrain your muscles to the new mechanics, the sooner you'll be doing better.

The key, then, is to quickly find the right program or the right approach to pitching so that you can make the most of your body's potential. It's essential for you to become a true student of the game. That means watching yourself on videotape to check your mechanics, closely observing major-league pitchers to see how they develop their mechanics, and of course, listening to and learning from your pitching coach. It's also essential that you have the courage to experiment with new approaches. It's too easy to try a new style once or twice and then chuck it simply because it doesn't feel right. Of course it's not going to feel perfect right away—you just started it!

Over the years, I've found that many pitchers are reluctant to change their style, for fear that a new suggestion might screw up their mechanics and ruin their next performance. But when you're young and just developing, you should experiment to develop the best pitching style you can.

MATURE ON THE MOUND MENTALLY

As we discussed earlier, most young athletes these days have heard about the mental rehearsal process called visualization. This mental technique, first developed and used by the East German Olympic team in the 1970s and popularized by such authors as Dr. Maxwell Maltz, is part of the neuromuscular control pattern that we just discussed. Pitchers, in particular, can develop markedly by using visualization.

Visualization employs your inner mind's "eye" to see yourself on the mound doing things perfectly. That means seeing yourself in a perfect motion, setting up batters perfectly, throwing perfect pitches, throwing a perfect game.

Most pitchers in pro ball take some time to work through the opponent's batting order mentally before they dress for the game. Then, when the game begins and the pitcher is on the mound facing the opposing team, he doesn't have to focus on distractions like pregame nervousness, poor weather, or a loud crowd. After all, the pitcher has already rehearsed and prepared for these distractions in his mind; the actual game situation appears to be routine. He's able to focus and concentrate on the game plan and not be distracted by the game scenery.

Does this process actually work? Does visualization help a pitcher concentrate on the batter? Consider that whenever I talk to a major-league pitcher just after he has completed a game, invariably he can easily and quickly recall every pitch he threw. It's as though he is reading from a script, but it's nothing more than total recall from his mind.

How can he do this? He was so focused on the game, so caught up in the flow of his performance, that his recall is practically instantaneous. Even more surprising, if you asked that pitcher whether he was distracted by the fight in the stands in the fourth inning or by the jets overhead in the sixth, he wouldn't necessarily recall those incidents at all. But ask him what kind of pitch he threw to Martinez in the second when the count was 3-and-2, and he'll give you a detailed recap of that pitch.

GETTING INTO THE FLOW

The concept of optimal flow is a relatively new one in the psychology of sport. The experience has always been there; it's just never had a scientific name.

You may know it as being in the zone, being focused, or being unconscious during the game. No matter what you call it, it's the sensation that you're aware only of the task at hand. In pitching, that means throwing strikes to one batter after another. Fireworks could be going off all around you, but you wouldn't even notice. Time seems to pass so quickly that you aren't even aware that you've been pitching for two or more hours. If you've had this wonderful experience in sports, then you know it's where you want to be when you're competing.

Here's the rub. Although scientists and psychologists know and recognize that optimal flow exists, nobody has yet figured out a way to get there. Sure, highly skilled performers— musicians, surgeons, and athletes—know all about the zone, of the great effects of being there. But there's no magic formula to get you there. Alas, for most people, flow just seems to come and go, depending on that day's situation.

That being said, some evidence shows that visualization exercises help induce flow states in athletes. That's another good reason to practice visualization. There's also some thought that having a regular routine before a performance helps get your brain ready to lock in on an optimal flow state.

The point is that once you get into the zone, you find that everything works just the way you planned or imagined it. If you're a pitcher, you find that you have perfect control of your pitches, that you have no need to make adjustments because everything is working so well. You seem to be on automatic pilot.

Once you've come down from a flow experience, it's much easier to recall the specific details of what happened to you during that self-hypnotic state. It's where you want to be in sports—living in the zone.

Don't worry if you don't reach optimal flow right away. Again, like all aspects of competitive sport, it takes time and experience. If you're a pitcher, you can obtain experience only by pitching. Indeed, few amateur pitchers have developed total recall of every pitch in every game. But when you do develop this mental skill of living in the zone, you know you're on your way to taking your game to a higher level.

IMPROVE YOUR CONTROL

Can visualization techniques really help you improve your control? Absolutely. In the same way that you prepare for each batter, you can use mental rehearsing to help you lock in your physical pitching mechanics to throw strike after strike.

Put it this way. If your current typical pattern is to throw one pitch high, the next pitch low, the next pitch outside and high, then you must sharpen your physical mechanics on the mound. There's too much fluctuation in your delivery, too many moving parts that aren't in sync. The only way to break out of that wildness mode is to reevaluate your mechanics, to shape them more appropriately, and then to develop your visualization pattern to reinforce your new delivery.

Theoretically, every young pitcher with a good arm and good physical ability should be able to throw strikes. However, and this goes back to observing major leaguers throw strikes, you'll find that the pitchers with the best control usually have the most compact, or most simple, windup.

First take a look at veteran pitcher Charlie Nagy. He practically never walks anybody, maybe one or two batters per nine

© VJ Sports Photography

A master of control, Charlie Nagy always finds his target.

innings. Now look at Nagy's delivery. It's practically nothing at all. He sets himself on the rubber, gets his target, mentally decides where he wants to locate the pitch, and delivers. True, Nagy is not the hardest thrower in the big leagues, but what he sacrifices in velocity he makes up with control and mastery of pitches. Besides, he throws hard enough to fool the batters, and that's all that matters.

There was a time in major-league baseball when all pitchers used big windups and big leg kicks. But over the last decade or so, most pitchers have realized that all that extra physical motion not only wasted strength and energy (especially on hot days) but also loused up their control. Most pitchers today go with a no-windup delivery. They find this style to be practical and efficient, and of course, it improves their ability to throw strikes.

If you want to improve your control, start with these guidelines:

Review Your Motion

Have the courage to evaluate and experiment with every part of your motion and delivery. See what parts you can simplify, particularly if they don't really serve any function in helping you on the mound (for example, hands-over-the-head windup, high leg kick, and so forth).

Try to Pinpoint Targets

Take a few moments each evening before you go to sleep to visualize yourself throwing pinpoint strikes. See yourself in as much detail as possible. See yourself in the perfect motion, and then see yourself throwing pitches to precise spots and locations. See yourself throwing perfect pitches at critical times in a game.

Don't just throw strikes over the plate—do better than that. Throw a pitch that's aimed at the catcher's left knee or in the lower right-hand corner of the batter's strike zone. See your curveball break sharply at the batter's shoulder and cut through the strike zone. Be precise. Get in the habit of mentally training your arm and body to respond to precise targets.

Divide the Strike Zone Into Quadrants

Divide the strike zone into four parts, or quadrants. Start thinking about how you're going to pitch to the various quadrants and how precise you can be in your delivery. That way, if you happen to miss throwing a strike into the lower-right quadrant by an inch or two, the pitch may land in the upper-right quadrant. You're still very much in the overall strike zone. By reshaping your delivery and by focusing on individual targets in the zone, you'll be on your way to improving your control dramatically.

Rehearse Mentally

Be certain to make the visualization process a daily part of your routine. As suggested, do it in the evening before you go to sleep. Remember, when it comes to visualizing perfect control on the mound, seeing really is believing.

Roger Clemens hurls the ball with great speed.

© Anthony Neste

DETERMINE THE BATTER'S THOUGHTS

If you're a pitcher and you can't remember the last time you put on a batting helmet and dug in at the plate, then you're missing out on an important experience. You can become a better pitcher only if you know what it's like to be a batter.

That may sound a bit odd, but let me explain. When you get down to basics, hitting is all about fear—or more precisely, about overcoming fear. All batters have an instinctive fear of being hit by a pitch. The reason? A ball going 80 to 90 miles per hour hurts when it hits you. Oh sure, you see big leaguers get hit, and they nonchalantly stroll down to first as though they were hit with a Wiffle ball. These guys are just too macho to let the pitcher know that being hit by his pitch hurt like hell.

The faster (and wilder) the pitcher is, the more fear the batter must overcome. If a pitcher doesn't throw real hard, the batter can dig in, knowing that he's got enough time to bail out if the pitch is headed his way. But if that's Randy Johnson on the mound and you're a left-handed batter, you know you have less than half a second to decide whether that next pitch is a perfect strike or a pitch that's coming for your head.

Few pitchers understand that fear is still the basis of pitching. If these pitchers had done more hitting as kids, they would know that and more often use fear as a tactic in their pitching technique.

PITCH INSIDE AND TIGHT

Learning how to pitch inside is essential to successful pitching. No, nobody is suggesting that you throw beanballs or try to hit people; that's ridiculous. But every successful pitcher in the big leagues will tell you that learning how to pitch inside to a batter is crucial.

Most batters can handle the pitch over the middle of the plate, and some batters prefer the pitch over the outside of the plate so that they can step into the pitch and drive it. Few batters like a pitch in close to the body. It makes them nervous. After all, an inch or two closer and they could be hit or get jammed on the hands.

As a pitcher, you can start to use a batter's fear to your advantage. Throw fastball strikes on the inside corner to back the batter off the plate a bit and make him a little less comfortable in the batter's box. Then you can start to work on him by throwing your off-speed pitches and breaking stuff away. Before too long, by following this pattern of inside-and-outside pitching, you have actually expanded the strike zone. Understandably, batters don't like that. Even tougher on the batters is that they can't really dig in at the plate because one of your inside fastballs might come too far inside.

Again, this is nothing more than employing a batter's instinctive fear of the pitched baseball to your advantage. That's why I say if you have ever batted in a game, you know the fear that batters have to cope with constantly. As a pitcher, you should always remember that.

LEARN ABOUT YOURSELF THROUGH OTHERS

One day in spring training a few years ago, I saw something I had never seen before. Paul Byrd, who was then in the Indians' farm system and is now with the New York Mets, was going around camp talking to the best hitters and best base runners.

Byrd, a crafty right-hander who had starred at Louisiana State, was "taking inventory," as he explained it to me. He figured that since he had never had a chance to bat against himself, he ought to go to the next best source—his teammates. Paul was asking his Indians teammates what they thought his best pitch was.

In spring training, of course, during the various intrasquad games, all the batters have a chance to face all the pitchers. Paul was interviewing his hitting teammates about what they thought of his pitches: How was my curveball? Was it sharp? Did it fool you? Did my motion tip off that a curve was coming? What about my fastball? Did it have good location? What about its movement? Paul asked questions to as many hitters as he could, under the assumption that who but the hitters could tell him about his pitches.

Then Paul would go through the same process with the better base stealers, to see what they thought of his move to first: Did I keep you tight to the bag? Did I tip off whether I was throwing to home or to first?

The more I saw this interrogation going on, the more I realized that Paul had a great idea. What makes more sense than talking with the "enemy" about your pitching, your motion, and so on? You come up with terrific information that you can use to make yourself into a more effective pitcher.

Now, during a high school or even a college season, you may not be able to chat with all your opponents. But you can certainly start with the players on your team. Talk to them about your pitches, in the same way that Paul Byrd talked with his teammates. You may be surprised by what you find out about yourself.

PREPARE FOR YOUR START ON THE MOUND

Putting on your game face is where it starts. Every pitcher does it. On the day of the game, as game time draws nearer, it seems that all pitchers like to be left alone so they can gather their thoughts and concentrate on the task at hand.

A game face, of course, is nothing more than an acknowledgment that the pitcher is becoming increasingly edgy, nervous, and eager to go to work. It's difficult for most athletes to sit around and do nothing, knowing that in a few hours they have to go out and expend themselves physically on the mound. So pitchers wait and pace, pace and wait, liked caged animals before feeding time.

When it's time to go, most pitchers follow a pregame ritual. That's fine; in fact, I tell young pitchers to start to develop one. I don't even object to superstitions, as long as they aren't dangerous or too complicated, and as long as they don't interfere with the pitcher's teammates. Most pitchers do go through a set pattern before each start, whether it's the time they start dressing, how they get dressed, how they stretch and loosen in the bullpen, or the T-shirt they wear. Players fall into superstitious patterns because they feel comfortable in those patterns. The comfort and confidence come from knowing that they did well after going through a particular routine and that they are going through the same ritual again.

This kind of simplistic, superstitious, cause-and-effect thinking pattern carries no scientific weight at all, but if it improves the pitcher's emotional sense of well-being that's all that matters. So feel free to have your own pregame routine, or even superstitions, as long as they make you feel comfortable and well prepared for the upcoming task.

Don't forget that these superstitious pregame rituals can extend to the entire team. Perhaps your ballclub goes through its pregame exercises in a certain stylized pattern before every game, or they wear the same practice jerseys in batting practice, or the guys sit in certain seats on the team bus for road games. These seemingly meaningless events can help breed team confidence and go a long way toward making the entire ballclub feel comfortable and relaxed before a game. That feeling can be instrumental in allowing the team to be sharp for that day's game.

GET RID OF THOSE FIRST-INNING JITTERS

Why is it? Why do so many excellent pitchers have problems in the first inning?

You know the pattern. The pitcher has difficulty in the first inning, either missing the strike zone or hanging his curveball or just not getting enough velocity on the fastball. The other team feasts on him, scoring a few runs. Then, in the following innings, the pitcher becomes unhittable. The longer the game lasts, the tougher he becomes. "Doggonit!" the pitching coach exclaims. "If I could just get you to start the second inning and not the first, you'd be throwing no-hitters every time out!"

Perhaps this happens to you. As I said, it's a very common problem for starting pitchers, and I'm always amazed that most pitchers don't know how to cope with it. They just shrug it off as "nerves" or "jitters" and let it go at that.

That's silly. It's my theory that most starting pitchers fall victim to first-inning jitters not because of anxiety but because they aren't loose yet. Oh sure—they've stretched and they've been in the bullpen warming up, but for some reason, starting pitchers seem to hold back in the bullpen and on the mound before the first batter steps in. It's as though they fear that if they really let her rip before they face that first batter that somehow they're going to wear themselves out before the game really starts.

It's an odd fear, because all these pitchers will tell you that they're in excellent shape and can easily pitch well into the night. But somehow—perhaps because they see each game as a long nine-inning journey—they want to conserve their energy and pace themselves by holding back early on. The irony is that by subconsciously trying to do that, they run the risk of not even lasting through that first inning.

Whenever I confront this situation, I urge the pitcher, as he's finishing his warm-up tosses, to really bear down and throw hard—as though the game had already started. To lock on to the upcoming game situation, it's not a bad idea to pretend that you're pitching to the first three batters. Set them up, throw strikes, and work on your out pitches. Once you're in the groove, you're ready to march in from the bullpen.

It's OK, and actually preferable, that you're sweating and working hard, because that's the way you want to be for the first batter. Remind yourself to continue throwing at top speed during your practice pitches (after you've become used to the pitching mound). You want to be ready and raring to go, already in midgame stride, when that lead-off batter steps in. Let *him* feel nervous and jittery; you're already in solid form.

This approach has worked many times for me in the past, and I strongly urge you to try it if you have difficulty with first-inning jitters. Look at the top relief pitchers in the majors, the guys who come in and throw gas. They heat up in the pen, get up to full throttle in a hurry, and stay at top speed until the call comes from the manager to come in and pitch. At that point, the closer sprints into the game and continues to throw gas in his warm-ups. He's in full form. He can't afford any jitters here; he has to throw strikes, right now, with superior velocity.

If this approach works for the top relief pitchers, who live on the edge and have to throw strikes immediately, then it ought to work for you as a starting pitcher. Try it.

MIX YOUR PITCHES

The key to pitching, at least at the higher levels, is keeping the batters off stride. Look at the best major-league pitchers. They win consistently because they have command of their pitches (they throw strikes) and because they mix up their pitches so batters don't know what's coming next. To do this, of course, you must have a few pitches to mix up. After all, if you throw only a fastball, you don't have much choice in your pitch selection.

But as you get older and develop your pitches, you will have to choose what to throw on each pitch. To my way of thinking—and I know many professional pitching coaches feel the same way—you ought to have a solid purpose for every pitch you throw. Don't throw a pitch without a reason; make every pitch count.

SETTING UP THE BATTER

As I mentioned earlier, you must rely on your pitching instincts and experience to size up each batter. As each opponent comes to the plate, you can quickly determine how far he stands from the plate, whether he looks like a power hitter or a slap hitter, whether he's using a large bat that he holds at the very end, whether he's choking up on the bat, and so on.

From there, develop a game plan for each batter. Ask yourself questions like these: Should I try to pitch him away? Should I pitch him tight and try to jam him? Or should I change speeds on each pitch so that he lunges?

Of course, you should be thinking about these issues with the full understanding that you want to throw strikes. It's extremely important to get ahead in the count. Because so many young hitters like to take a pitch, your best bet is to throw a fastball down the middle as the first pitch. Oh sure, there are some hitters who will be waiting to smack that first one. But odds are that the batter will be taking. If you throw a fastball for a strike, right away you're ahead of the batter, and then you can really go to work on him.

Let's assume then that the count is no balls and one strike. This gives you a chance to experiment with your pitches. You could throw a curve, a slider, maybe even try a sinker or forkball. As you get more experience, you'll learn that a change-up is often effective. The sooner you learn how to throw these various pitches—and throw them for strikes—the more effective a pitcher you'll become.

Of course, the only way to master these pitches (especially if you're still in high school) is to work on them. You can try different pitches in your bullpen sessions, when you're shagging flies in the outfield, when you're having a catch with a teammate, or when you happen to be pitching in a lopsided game.

Don't lose your courage when throwing new pitches. Maybe you'll bounce a few change-ups in front of the catcher. Perhaps an opposing batter will smack a hanging curve for a homer. Hey—that happens. If you decide never to throw that pitch again, you're already defeated. Don't remove a major weapon from your arsenal.

Some years ago, when Frank Viola was developing his pitching style in the minor leagues, he was taught by his pitching coach in Class AA ball, Johnny Podres, how to throw a change-up. Viola didn't get the hang of it at first, and besides, he had always had a great fastball and curve in college, so he wasn't sure he needed a change-up.

But Podres convinced Viola that if he ever wanted to get to the big leagues, he had to have at least three pitches, and the change was a perfect match. So Frank went to work on the pitch, and worked on it all the time, including in his bullpen sessions. Finally, the day came when Frank decided to use the new pitch in a game, and sure enough, he got to just the right

Add a change-up to your pitching arsenal. It worked for Frank Viola.

© Anthony Neste

batter to throw it to. Problem was, Frank didn't get the pitch down enough in the strike zone, and the batter promptly hit Viola's new pitch about 400 feet over the left-field wall.

Afterward, Frank was approached by Podres, who was curious about whether Frank was going to give up on the new pitch after seeing that it was hit into the next county. To Viola's credit, he shrugged it off and told Podres that it wasn't the pitch's fault, it was just that he hadn't mastered it yet. Frank soon learned how to throw the change effectively, so effectively that it catapulted him to the big leagues. Viola became a successful pitcher and eventually won a Cy Young award.

The lesson here? Don't give up on a pitch just because things don't happen instantaneously for you. These things take time, and you might have to take a few lumps early on before circumstances turn around. And be sure to experiment with different pitches before deciding which ones are going to work (or not work) for you.

THE ART OF MAKING ADJUSTMENTS

You know the feeling. You're in a tough jam on the mound. With runners on second and third, you know you have to throw the next batter nothing but curves and changes. After all, he's a dead-on fastball hitter with power, and you don't want to give in to his strength.

The problem is that the last couple of curves you threw bounced at about 55 feet and you walked a batter. The last change-up you delivered was hit into the gap for a clean double. That's why you have men on second and third.

You know you have to throw that curve and change. You know you have the guts to throw them. But how do you make that fine-tuning adjustment on the mound during the game so that you don't bounce more pitches? How do you do it when you're in a tight spot, with men on second and third?

"Adjustment" is the operative word. As you go higher in the game, that's all you hear pitchers say: "I have to make some adjustments out there." To do this, you must know every feeling, every sensation, every touch of how you deliver a perfect pitch. You should know exactly what it feels like when you snap off a dynamite curve, throw a wonderfully deceptive change, or pop a hard fastball.

It's something like visualization. You know, from a neuro-muscular point of view, the physical motions you perform when you deliver a perfect pitch. It's like having little sensors in your body. You recognize, for example, that your motion begins a certain way, that you kick your leg in a certain style, that your arm and arm velocity are precise, and that you hold and deliver the ball a particular way. By checking these system sensors, you should be able to pinpoint the problem with your pitches. Once you determine what you need to adjust, to fine-tune, you can make the change.

Many pitchers find that they hang a curve because they're letting the pitch go too early in their delivery. Likewise, if they're bouncing it, they're holding the ball too long. Perhaps they're not pushing off the rubber properly, and it's affecting their mechanics. A pitcher may sometimes hang a curve when the ball is new and relatively slippery and simply slips off his fingers.

Whatever the reason, you see the results. Here's where you can really establish yourself as a young but mature pitcher. Many youngsters begin to panic on the mound, and instead of calmly trying to figure out what's not working, they fidget, play with the rosin bag, argue with the umpire, or take too much time between pitches, as though stalling is going to help them perform better.

From a coach's perspective, these are all telltale signs that a pitcher is losing his focus and the ability to make an adjustment. Pitchers are surprised when they're lifted from the game when this happens. "Hey, skip, my arm's not tired!" is what they always say. What the young pitcher doesn't understand is that the manager's decision to take him out has to do not with fatigue but with his inability to make the necessary adjustments to stay in control of his game.

Here's another little secret you should know. Few high school or college coaches know how to teach their pitchers the art of making adjustments. It's pretty much an intuitive process that you have to develop on your own. As I mentioned, it has to do with viewing your body as a physical machine that has all sorts of little checkpoints and checks and balances that keep everything in sync. If something isn't functioning properly, you must identify it and be able to make adjustments quickly without panicking.

Another example. I once had an outstanding young pitcher who always had great stuff when he kept his arm in a three-quarter delivery style. Sometimes though, by the fifth or sixth inning, his arm slot would drop down a bit, so that his delivery was getting closer to sidearm than three-quarters. When he did that, all his pitches would become flat and easy to hit.

I would sit with him between innings and explain to him about his arm slot, about how he was dropping his arm down. Even though he knew he shouldn't be doing that, he didn't sense it for himself. As a result, he couldn't make the adjustment. He would have to ask me whether he was dropping his arm down, and only after I told him that he was dropping down would he try to adjust.

I knew that until he learned how to sense this problem for himself, he would never be able to go more than a few innings. And he would have problems at the next level of ball. After all, being able to sense your delivery problems is just as important as being able to make the adjustments. You can't always rely on your coach to "sense" those problems for you.

A CHECKLIST OF ADJUSTMENT TECHNIQUES

To make proper adjustments, you have to know what's working for you. Keep these thoughts in mind when you pitch:

- Know what feels comfortable and right for you when you're pitching well. Keep a diary of what has worked for you in the past, especially during critical times in a game, and review it before you pitch.

- If you have to start making adjustments during a game, don't panic. Instead, pinpoint the problem first, and then make the adjustment. Do it coolly, calmly, and scientifically.

- Never make dramatic changes in your style of pitching or mechanics during the game. That will only make the problem worse.

- Learn how to sense the parts of your pitching mechanics that have to work for you. Remember that you will seldom pitch an entire game in which you won't have to make adjustments. Look upon the process as a challenge, from both a physical and mental point of view.

WHAT IF THEY MAKE ERRORS BEHIND YOU?

One quick word about errors. You wouldn't be the first pitcher in baseball who has made all the right pitches and all the right adjustments only to see weakly hit ground balls and loopy fly balls mishandled by your teammates.

Of course, this is frustrating to any pitcher, but remember that miscues and bobbles in the field are just as frustrating to your teammates, especially to the teammate who made the error. The last thing you want to do on the mound is show your displeasure or anger at such an event.

Instead, you just draw up your pants and pride and go back to work. You start working on the next batter. It's as simple as that.

I remember playing second base in the minors and making an error on a routine grounder. The pitcher, who was new to the team, fussed and fumed and threw his rosin bag in disgust at my misplay. Now, nobody felt worse about the error than I did, and the last thing I needed to see was the pitcher showing his disgust.

So I called time, strolled over to the mound, and said to the pitcher, "Jim, I know I muffed that grounder, and I apologize. It was my fault." He sneered down at me as though I *owed* him an apology. So then I said to him, "I'll tell you what. The next time you walk a batter, which is *your* fault, I'll expect you to come over to second base and apologize to me. Got it, hotshot?"

He got the message.

THE SECOND GO-ROUND

The mental chess match that goes on between pitcher and hitter can continue for years. Every time you face a batter, you should log that experience in your brain's computer. The batter is certainly doing the same thing, keeping a full working encyclopedia of every at-bat he's had against you, what you threw him, what he hit well, what he swung at and missed, and so on.

Let's assume you retired Brown in his first at-bat in the first inning by getting him to chase a tempting fastball that was a little high. After he swung and missed for strike three, you knew he was angry at himself for chasing a bad pitch.

Now, here comes Brown in the fourth inning. You can be certain he's not going to swing at a high fastball again—or if he does, it will be at a pitch he can handle. Knowing this, why not tempt him with fastballs away? See if he'll chase those. Or throw him some curves that break to the outside corner. Then, when he's convinced you're going to try to throw that rising fastball past him again, throw your change-up. Remember, he's waiting on that burning fastball, so when you throw the tempting change, don't be surprised if he pops it up, or is so befuddled that he swings right through it. That's the beauty of changing speeds.

This kind of mental chess game continues for the rest of the game and continues for each batter. Sometimes, the batter is going to outfox you, and he'll get his hit. Most of the time, though, you'll outsmart him, simply because you have the advantage of knowing what pitch you're going to throw next. Theoretically, you can get to the point where you can outsmart every batter you face. That's a worthy goal to shoot for.

POSTGAME ANALYSIS

One of the most important aspects of taking your game to the next level is knowing how to conduct an objective, and beneficial, postgame analysis of your performance. You don't have to do this analysis immediately after the game. But, you should think about your performance within a few hours after the game has come to an end, so that all the game's details are still very fresh in your mind.

With Yourself

Most young pitchers don't know how to analyze their performance. Instead, they concentrate on the stats of the day—how many innings, pitches, walks, strikeouts, earned runs, and so on. That's fine for younger pitchers. But as you get older, you should be able to reflect on each critical point in the game and review in your mind what kinds of pitches you threw and why. Did you make the right decision? Did you make the proper adjustments? Did anything about your pitching surprise you?

These are the kinds of questions you should be asking yourself. Be analytical. Try to dissect every pitching performance, and find something that you can use in your next game. Maybe it was the way you set up a batter, or a certain pitch you used as an out pitch. The point is that you should build upon each performance.

What if you just had a bad outing on the mound? Shouldn't you just write that one off, forget about it? Many coaches will tell you to do just that. The problem is that if you don't analyze why you did so poorly, then you aren't doing anything to prevent it from happening again. When you have several bad outings, your coach must assume that this is no fluke, that you really aren't an effective pitcher.

So my advice to you is to take the time to analyze a poor showing. Was it your mechanics? Did you not make the adjustments? Be careful of blaming your performance on the umpire, the mound, and so on. Those are poor excuses. You must make the adjustments in order to survive on the mound.

With Your Coach

Most smart coaches know that there's little sense in talking objectively with you just after you've performed. They know that you're still pumped up with adrenaline and that your mind and body are still heavily focused on the game. As a result, it doesn't do much good to try to dissect your game.

The smarter coaches will wait to talk with you the next day, after you've calmed down a bit and can reflect more objectively on the game. From there, the coach should go over each inning with you, asking why you threw particular pitches and what your thinking was. He should be able to recall the original game plan and analyze how close you came to executing it.

Don't view these sessions as hurtful or damaging. Try to look upon them as being helpful. A coach who levels with you can help you develop as a pitcher. If you just want to hear how well you pitched, well, you can hear that from your friends and family. That's their responsibility. But if you really want to learn about your performance, this is the time.

Put aside your personal feelings, and listen and learn. Don't be defensive. Don't make excuses. Just pay attention and try to learn for the next performance.

Remember always that pitching is a complex physical and psychological act that requires stamina, intelligence, strength, and intestinal fortitude. Becoming a successful pitcher involves a lot of work, but it can be an enjoyable, and profitable, ride.

8

MASTERING THE MENTAL SIDE OF HITTING

We've already discussed the physical side of hitting. It may seem easy—keep your weight back, extend your arms, hold your head steady, and so forth. But every hitter knows that frustration is the name of this game. The sooner you come to understand that the life of a hitter is a hard one, the sooner you can begin to extract some fun from this game.

Now, that last sentence may seem a bit contradictory, but it's true. Once you get to the point where you understand that hitting is full of frustration, then you can start to focus on your strengths as a hitter and begin to enjoy your accomplishments.

Think of it for a moment. First off, it's very difficult to perfect your swing. It takes weeks, months, years of hitting off a batting tee, hitting soft toss, strengthening your wrists, and taking batting practice—and that's just to get rid of built-in flaws like hitches and lunges and other habits that can mess up your stroke.

Then, once you've mastered the mechanics of your swing, you have to go out and do it in a game. That means standing in the batter's box, facing a pitcher who's only 60 feet away throwing a rock-like sphere at up to 100 miles per hour. The pitcher hopes to throw strikes, but who knows? He may let one slip toward your body. So a certain amount of physical danger and fear is involved in the art of hitting.

To make it more challenging, the pitcher can make the ball do different things. It can curve, dip, slide, slow down, and drop. And, of course, he does these things without telling you. (By the way, back in the early days of baseball, in the late 1800s, the batters were permitted to dictate to the pitchers where and how they would throw every pitch! Unfortunately for hitters today, those days are long gone.)

Finally, let's assume you do everything perfectly well. You have a great swing at a pitch, and you gain that momentary inner satisfaction as the bat meets the ball solidly, only to see an outfielder race over and make a wondrous diving catch of your line shot. All you get for your effort is an 0-for-1.

THE ZEN OF BASEBALL

Why am I telling you all this? Because in the Zen-like world of baseball, mastery of hitting a ball is, at best, an ethereal, day-to-day occurrence. Just because you do it today doesn't guarantee that the same magic will happen again tomorrow, or for that matter, on your next at-bat.

What does all this mean? In short, few actions in sport involve as much pure concentration as hitting a baseball. Even the most minor distraction can affect your stroke. One thing, however, is for sure. The more you practice your swing, the closer you come to obtaining that sense of perfection at the plate. Of course, no batter has ever been perfect; no one has come close to hitting every pitch perfectly. But if you work at it long enough, you'll be amazed at how much more proficient you'll become with the bat.

COPE WITH FRUSTRATION

While it's nice to talk and dream about becoming a Zen master with your hitting stroke, in the real world you'll have to deal with frustration more than you'd like. As we all know, the best hitters in the game fail most of the time.

But that's not the point. The best hitters in the game learn to cope with their frustration, to keep their emotions in check, and to look at the hitting experience as a chance to evaluate every swing scientifically. Talk to any major-league hitters— and these are the best in the business—and they'll tell you that you won't start becoming a better hitter until you put anger behind you and start thinking scientifically.

What do I mean by "frustration"? I refer specifically to those situations in which you are so upset by your performance at the plate that you feel compelled to throw your helmet, shriek obscenities, or argue with the umpire. Maybe you take your hitting woes out into the field with you and allow a bad at-bat to affect your defensive play. Or perhaps you take the game home with you, and spend the nights calculating your sinking batting average and worrying about your next day's performance. Your mood swings become noticeable to your family and friends; they can tell how you did in a game just by the way you carry yourself around the neighborhood or the house.

As you might imagine, this isn't the way major leaguers conduct themselves. True, major leaguers are guilty of many sins, such as occasionally hotdogging on the field, or being greedy, or whatever, but when it comes to coping with the daily frustrations of the game, they've learned those lessons long ago.

Brook Jacoby, for years a rock-steady, hard-hitting third baseman for the Indians, was recognized by his peers for always keeping an even temper—through hot streaks and cold streaks alike. I once asked Brook how he learned this essential lesson about the game.

"I remember when I was in junior high," replied Jake. "I used to go nuts if I didn't do well in a game, and I would become moody and sullen. But then one day, my Dad told me in no uncertain terms that if I wanted to keep on playing baseball, I would have to learn to keep my emotions under control—that by giving in to my emotions, I was making myself a worse player, not a better one."

That's a valuable insight, and it's one every young player should start to learn. Giving in to your emotions does two negative things:

1. It shows everybody on the field that you're angered with your last at-bat, that you didn't succeed, and that you're giving into that "I failed; therefore I'm angry" syndrome. To any scouts who are watching, this could be a tip-off that you're not mentally mature enough to sign a pro contract or move on to a higher level of ball.

2. Once you let your emotions control you, you lose control of your well-practiced, well-rehearsed approach to hitting. Anger only gets in the way of your achieving your goals.

Let me explain. Let's say you're fooled badly by a curveball. If you throw a temper tantrum, then your mind and body focus on having a fit. What you should really be thinking about is why you were fooled by that curve and how you can make the adjustment so you aren't fooled again. As you might imagine, making the proper adjustment calls for a calm approach, not a tantrum.

CONTROL YOUR EMOTIONS

There is no question that you must learn to control your emotions. So here's a little advice that I've given ballplayers for years.

Make a deal with yourself. Give yourself exactly five seconds after each at-bat to feel and vent your emotions. Whether you strike out or hit a home run, whether you pop up or get a base hit, give yourself a window of exactly five seconds to express your emotions.

Here's the catch. Once those five seconds have elapsed, that's it. You can't allow any of your emotions to come through. The clock starts ticking immediately, so you can't postpone those five seconds. Once the time is up, you have to maintain yourself and carry yourself like a real pro.

Try that approach during your next few games. Remember that five seconds doesn't last too long. Once it's gone, you've got to be a pro. Do major leaguers do this? You bet. Two good examples of players who keep their emotions in check are Jeff Bagwell of the Astros and Mike Piazza of the Dodgers. Whether they hit one into the upper deck or strike out with the bases loaded, they keep their emotional level under control.

A BATTING SLUMP: WHAT IT REALLY MEANS

There's always been a lot of talk, and a lot of theory, about batting slumps and how to get out of them. But before you start turning your attention to curing a slump, you first have to define what a slump is—and isn't.

Let's take two games as examples. In one game, you go to bat four times. On your first at-bat, you get jammed by a pitch and hit a weak flare for a base hit. On your second at-bat, you get fooled by a curve, make weak contact, and get on with a swinging bunt. Then, on your third at-bat, you check your swing and hit a pitch that barely loops over the first baseman's head. On your fourth at-bat, your seeing-eye grounder makes it through the infield for another hit. So, as far as the box score (and your batting average) is concerned, you went 4-for-4—a perfect day!

In game two, you come to the plate four times and are not once fooled by a pitch. You line out hard to third base, hit a deep fly ball to center that's caught near the wall, hit a one-hop bullet to the shortstop, and, on your last at-bat, your sinking line drive is snatched off the grass by a diving right fielder. Another day at the ballpark, another 0-for-4. You go home with nothing to show for your day's efforts.

But let me ask you this: Of the two performances, which sounds more like a slump? If just getting hits means you're not in a slump, that first game is fine. But from a professional hitter's point of view, the second game is the better effort, by far. Why? You were just lucky—flat-out lucky—to get on base in game one. If the goal of hitting is to avoid being fooled by the pitcher and to hit the ball hard, then you failed. In contrast, in game two you hit rockets every at-bat, even if your batting average fell a few points.

Here's the key: All pro players, coaches, and scouts know that over a season, the batter who consistently hits the ball hard will have a high batting average. It makes no difference whether you go hitless on a particular day, because in the long run you're going to have many days when those line drives aren't caught.

LOOK FOR A QUALITY AT-BAT

Some batting coaches in pro ball go so far as to gauge each at-bat as being quality or nonquality in form. Coaches use the distinction to educate and inform the batter about whether he was ready and prepared for each appearance at the plate, whether he was off balance, whether he was fooled by pitches, or whether he even had any good swings.

The idea behind a quality at-bat rating is a solid one. Rather than judge your performance on whether you got a hit or made an out, you now evaluate each plate appearance by whether you or the pitcher was in command.

Now, this kind of rating doesn't always jibe with your batting average. You might have four quality at-bats in a game, but have no hits to show for it. Conversely, you might collect four scratch hits, but have no quality at-bats. Let's say that you have four at-bats in a game and you do the following:

First at-bat: After falling behind in the count 0-2, you foul off several pitches until you finally draw a base on balls.

Second at-bat: After going ahead in the count 2-0, you get an off-speed pitch that you hit as a high fly ball to center field.

Third at-bat: With the count at 2-2, the pitcher throws you a hard slider. You're able to reach out and slap the ball the opposite way for a flare that happens to fall in for a hit.

Fourth at-bat: Facing a tough relief pitcher, you line a shot that's just barely foul on the first pitch. On the second pitch, you swing over a sharp curveball. You take the third pitch just inside for a ball. On the fourth pitch, you hit a solid one-hopper directly at the shortstop, who quickly converts the ball into an out.

How would you judge these at-bats? Well, according to the official scorebook, you would have been 1-for-3 with a walk. All things considered, that's a decent day's work—a .333 batting average.

Now, look at each at-bat from a quality point of view. On the first at-bat, you had to work out of a deep hole of 0-2 to get a walk. That means you were sharp at the plate, didn't swing at any tempting pitches, and transformed that potential strikeout into a positive—you got on base. That's a quality at-bat.

On the second at-bat, it's true that you got ahead in the count. But you were then fooled by an off-speed pitch and you lofted a high fly ball—an easy out—to the center fielder. That's not a quality at-bat.

On the third time at the plate, the pitcher threw you a tough pitch on the outside corner. If you had taken the pitch, you would have struck out. If you had tried to pull it, you would have hit an easy grounder, also an out. Instead, you waited on it, and did the only thing you could with it—you slapped the pitch the other way for a hit. True, it may not have been a solid line drive, but you got enough bat on the ball to make it count. That's an excellent piece of hitting—working with what the pitcher has dealt you—and that's a quality at-bat.

On the fourth trip to the plate, you knew the relief pitcher was good and you were ready for him. You got in some excellent strokes, and when you did hit the ball fair, you hit a one-hop shot to the infield. Yes, the infielder made the one-hopper into an out, but if you had hit the ball anywhere except right at him, you would have had a hit. Chalk this one up as a quality at-bat too.

In sum, you had three quality at-bats out of four chances. That's considerably better than .333. So by any professional standards, you had a terrific day at the plate.

KEEPING TRACK OF YOUR QUALITY AT-BATS

At the conclusion of each game you should keep a diary of every at-bat. Remember that you're not interested here in whether you got a hit or what your batting average is; as explained above, you can have four poor at-bats yet come away with four hits. Instead you should be judging here whether each at-bat was a quality one or whether it was not up to your hitting potential.

After each game, describe briefly whether and why each at-bat was a quality one or not.

Game date

At-bat # 1—A quality at-bat because I took the pitcher deep into the count and then lined a one-hopper right at the shortstop.

At-bat # 2—Not a quality at-bat. I got fooled by a breaking pitch, which I popped up to second. Didn't wait long enough on the curve.

At-bat # 3—A quality at-bat because I waited on the same curve that I popped up last at-bat and drilled it to the gap for a double.

In sum: By keeping track of quality at-bats you can, after a while, figure out whether you're seeing the ball well at the plate or whether you might be heading into a slump. The point is not to worry so much about your batting average, but instead to concentrate on making every at-bat a quality one. The more quality at-bats you have, the more hits you'll have.

Ultimately, if you have consistently good quality at-bats your batting average will rise to a high level.

These distinctions between your quality at-bats and your daily batting average are important because there may be little correlation between the two. You may have a high batting average but relatively few quality at-bats. Likewise, you could have a low batting average with many quality at-bats.

The beauty of the quality at-bat evaluation is that you don't even think about making any changes in your stroke or stance unless you have a string of poor at-bats. If you're getting top-notch swings and you're making solid contact—even if your batting average doesn't show it—don't give in to the temptation of making changes.

That's not always easy to do. But in the long run, you'll benefit more by looking at your quality at-bats rather than your batting average. The more honest you are about your quality at-bats, the better you'll swing the bat. The upshot is this: If you have consistently good quality at-bats, your batting average will rise to a high level.

WHERE SLUMPS BEGIN

Every baseball coach has a theory about how and why batting slumps begin. I have one too. In my opinion, a batting slump starts when you're hitting well!

Let me explain. Start with a batter who's doing well at the plate. He's hitting the ball well, seeing it well, not getting fooled, and his batting average is way up there. The batter is feeling very comfortable at the plate.

Perhaps, though, the batter has gotten a bit too comfortable. I've watched pro players for years. A player doing well at bat always says that he's "seeing the ball real well," that he's not getting fooled. The ball is easy to see and easy to follow.

During a slump, the same batter will tell you that he's not seeing the pitch well, that he's lunging at pitches, and that he's off balance in his stride. The batter will say, "You know, I got a fastball right down the middle, but instead of hitting a line drive up the middle—like I did last week—this time, I fouled the pitch back. I just missed it."

A batter who has been waiting well on curveballs and hitting them hard to the opposite field is now pulling those same curveballs into easy grounders. "I can't understand it," says the batter. "I don't understand why I'm not hitting that pitch well."

If you have enough at-bats like these, where you get your pitch but don't hit the ball well, before too long you convince yourself that you're in a slump. For too many hitters, that means going through a wholesale reevaluation of their batting stroke plus endless hours of misery and worry.

Let's back up a step. Remember when things were going fine, and you were seeing the ball well? It's my theory that ballplayers set the wheels in motion for a slump when they become too relaxed at the plate. Instead of seeing that pitch all 60 feet, 6 inches, they start to assume that the pitch is going to be a good one and swing at it.

It's almost as though the batter has been seeing previous pitches all the way to the plate. Because of that intense concentration, he's "seeing the ball well" and "not getting cheated" on his swings. But let's assume that the batter is "seeing the ball" only 40 feet, or only 35 feet, on its way to the plate. By seeing the ball only 40 feet, I mean that instead of concentrating on the pitch all the way, the batter merely assumes it's going to be in a good spot to hit and swings at it. How many times have you (or a batter you've watched) taken your eyes off the pitch by jerking your head around at the last second? Don't forget that the most important element in hitting is keeping your eye on the ball; yet even major leaguers often fall victim to taking their vision away from the flight of the pitch.

Hence, if the batter's assumption that the pitch is going to be perfect is off by just a little bit, then his swing is going to be off just a little bit too. That would explain why a batter would wonder how yesterday he could crush the same pitch that he merely fouled off today. It explains how he pulled that pitch to short, rather than waiting on it and slapping it to right field. The batter's assumption that a perfect pitch is coming explains any combination of things that could screw up his perfect stroke.

AND NOW, FOR THE REALLY BAD NEWS . . .

Here's the scary part. Instead of keeping his hard-earned stroke intact and focusing on each pitch all 60 feet, a batter may panic and start tinkering with his swing. He asks his coaches what's wrong. He asks his teammates on the bench to watch his stroke to see if something is flawed. Before you know it, a batter who has a perfectly good stroke makes all sorts of drastic changes and modifications. This really puts him in a slump, when all he had to do was concentrate more on each pitch all the way to the plate.

In sum, just be very careful when it comes to changing your swing and stance. Make certain that you make all the easy adjustments (like focusing on the pitch) first before you start reinventing your entire swing.

MAKE SOMETHING GOOD HAPPEN

This expression is an outgrowth of having a quality at-bat. It simply means that when you come to the plate, recognize that you're on offense. It's your job to make something good happen for you and your team. Whether that means swinging away for a hit, putting down a sacrifice bunt, or angling for a base on balls, you—not the pitcher—should be in command of the at-bat.

To accomplish this goal, you have to be watching and observing the pitcher, and putting together your game plan. What kind of pitcher is this? Does he throw hard? What kind of curve does he have? Does he have a hard time getting the ball in the strike zone? Can I bunt on him? Does he tip off his pitches?

These are the kinds of questions you should have answered for yourself while you were in the on-deck circle or sitting on the bench. Too many young players warm up in the on-deck circle by swinging bats and chatting with their teammates or looking into the stands for their girlfriends. They don't even take a look at the pitcher to see what he's got!

Remember: Pitchers are creatures of habit. They often unconsciously repeat their pitching sequence to each batter so that they can keep themselves in a groove. If you watch closely enough, you'll see patterns begin to evolve. A pitcher might always start out with a fastball for strike one, then a curve for strike two, and then a change-up for strike three. Or you'll notice that on a 3-2 count, the pitcher always throws a fastball.

These are the kinds of patterns and tip-offs you should be watching for. The more you know about the pitcher's tendencies, the easier it's going to be for you to make something good happen.

Al Goldis, the director of scouting for the Reds and an expert on hitting, says that all a player has to do is hit the ball hard twice a game. If you get four at-bats in a game, you might end up with a strikeout and a groundout for two of your at-bats. If you hit the ball hard on your other two at-bats, chances are good that at least one of those hard-hit balls will become a base hit, and maybe both will become hits.

This is Goldis' way of trying to take pressure off a young hitter. Sure, you *try* to hit the ball hard every at-bat, but give the pitcher some credit. He's trying to get you out—and he's got eight fielders behind him to help. But if you do succeed in hitting the ball hard twice a game, over time you'll accumulate a number of games in which you go 2-for-4.

So, depending upon how you define a slump, you can go in different directions. To me though, a batting slump doesn't start with an 0-for-4, or even an 0-for-8. You have to be a careful and objective judge of whether you're making solid contact with the pitch. If you are making good contact, then you have to be courageous and weather the storm until your next hit comes. If you're doing things right at the plate, then your next hit has a good chance of arriving on your next at-bat. Just make certain you don't fidget, fool around, or tinker with your batting stance or stroke.

If you're making good contact, questioning your stroke and making alterations will only louse up what you're doing well. That's not to say that you won't be tempted to change things—after all, you haven't got a hit—but keep your emotions out of it. If you're swinging well, just be patient.

On the other hand, if you don't feel comfortable at the plate, or if you're not making good contact, then you have to be honest about that too. Ask yourself to be more precise: Why does my swing feel like it's off? What can I do to adjust it properly? Be careful with your tinkering. Don't be tempted to make wholesale changes because you're temporarily frustrated.

Remember that anytime you make major changes in your stroke, it's going to take several at-bats before your body feels comfortable with those changes. Whether it's moving your hands back farther, choking up on the bat, moving your feet in your stance, or another kind of change, it rarely works perfectly on your next at-bat. It takes some time, and some more at-bats, before those changes begin to kick in.

THE FIFTY AT-BATS FORMULA

I remember talking to Indians slugger Manny Ramirez when he was struggling with his batting average in the low minors. He told me that every day he felt pressured to get at least a 1-for-4, or even better, a 2-for-4. He explained that in high school, when he played only three games a week, he could keep focused on every at-bat.

Now, in pro ball, where he played every night, it was difficult to keep hitting all the time. After going hitless for a few nights, Manny's batting average would tumble, and he felt even more pressure to get a hit.

I suggested to Ramirez that he stop keeping track of his daily performance and instead start focusing on every 25 or 50 at-bats. "You see, Manny," I explained to him, "You know that over the course of 25 at-bats you're going to get at least 10 hits. You're just too good a hitter. So, to get rid of the daily 0-for-4 pressure, just concentrate on blocks of 25 at-bats and look for 10 hits during that time. And when you get 10 hits, you'll be hitting .400."

This new approach worked wonders for Manny, and he's now learned to get away from the daily pressure and to focus only on the long-range picture of hitting.

KEEP A DIARY TO STAY ON TRACK

You've probably heard on a telecast that many major leaguers keep a diary of each pitcher in the league. It's true. Some hitters, like Albert Belle, keep extensive diaries of each pitcher, which they refer to every day.

© VJ Sports Photography

Albert Belle keeps elaborate diaries of each pitcher he faces.
He knows what to expect.

It's a good habit for you to start. Now, in the league you play in, you might not see the same pitchers repeatedly as big leaguers do, but you can keep track of your daily performance. I'm not concerned here about your batting average, but about the mechanics of your swings—whether you felt good at the plate, whether you hit the ball hard, whether you were fooled by a pitch, and so on.

The more you can remember and write down about each performance, the more you'll learn about yourself, about the patterns you go through, and about the adjustments that work for you. Such a diary becomes a wonderful book to review in the off-season as well, because you can pinpoint the nuances of your stance and swing that you might otherwise have forgotten over the long, cold winter months.

Of course, you should keep track of the other parts of your game, including your base running, your defensive play, and if relevant, your pitching performances. Most ballplayers study videotape of their performances endlessly. That's helpful, but the dedicated ballplayer will find that keeping a personal performance diary is an even bigger help.

TAKE COMMAND OF YOUR AT-BATS

Some young batters approach the plate in a defensive mode. I find that odd, because a batter is supposed to be on offense, not defense.

It's not that these hitters aren't serious about their hitting, or that they don't hope to get a hit. No, not at all; in fact, many of these young hitters work long and hard hours at improving their strokes. But when the moment of truth comes, they tend to put so much pressure on themselves that they practically defeat themselves on the way to the plate. All the pitcher has to do is wind up and throw strikes.

Why does this phenomenon occur? Simple. Imagine working hard and long to reach your goal, only to realize that you'll have just a few chances to show your stuff during the course of a game. Psychological studies show that when a young hitter faces a pitcher in a game situation, his pulse usually skyrockets, and nervous anxiety becomes a major part of his performance. The batter must defeat not only the pitcher but also his own nervous anxiety.

DON'T FIGHT YOUR NERVES

I have just two pieces of advice for young hitters dealing with this anxiety. First, understand and accept that you're going to be nervous. Don't fight it; just understand that it's there. Many pro hitters, in fact, look forward to nervous anxiety. As one major leaguer once told me, "If I weren't a little bit nervous about hitting, then I'd really be nervous! After all, when those little jitters fill my stomach, that's my assurance that my body is set and ready for action. It's primed and ready to work. Without that nervousness, I'd be worried that I wasn't ready for action. Maybe too laid back, and as a result, not ready to bat."

Perhaps you haven't heard that insight before, but it's one worth remembering: Don't fight your nerves. Recognize that your nervousness means your body is ready for action.

The second piece of advice is this: When you get into the batter's box, put your hitting stroke on automatic pilot. You've heard this advice before in the book, but it's so important that it bears repeating. When the pitch is on the way, all you have time to do is figure out whether it's a strike or a ball, and whether you should swing at it. Be primitive in your approach. Don't clutter your head with thoughts and concerns about your stance or hand position or where your weight is. Just see the ball and swing. Let your instinctive athletic ability take over. You can make adjustments *between* pitches, but don't try it *during* the pitch.

Above all, whether you finish your at-bat with a home run or a strikeout, you should return to the bench with a feeling that you were ready and that you let her rip at the plate. That's all you can ask for when you hit.

The best part is that once you start to believe in this simple Zen-like philosophy, you'll begin to control your nervous energy and get good swings on each at-bat. You'll find that your defensiveness at the plate has been replaced by a feeling of self-confidence—that you, not the pitcher, are in control of your at-bats.

Pete Rose, who holds the record for most hits in a major-league career, used to say that when he got into the batter's box, the only thing he focused on was getting the fat part of the bat on the ball. That was his way of trying to eliminate the clutter in his mind so that he could focus on the task at hand. Every major leaguer has found a way of doing this; you too must find a way.

Take a look at pure power. When Frank Thomas bats, he transfers his power by fully extending his arms as he makes contact with the ball.

BECOME A SMART HITTER

A resourceful, clever hitter has both the experience to recognize situations and the ability to execute skills. Here are several examples of smart hitters in action:

1. As the runner on first breaks for second, the batter waits just long enough on an outside pitch to slap it to right field, thus executing a perfect hit-and-run.

2. The leadoff batter watches the pitcher warm up. The batter's team is down by two runs late in the game. He notices that the pitcher is having difficulty throwing strikes. The batter patiently works a walk out of the tiring pitcher to get a rally started.

3. Observing a new pitcher coming into the game, the batter sees that the pitcher is breaking his curveball

into the dirt in front of the plate. The hitter simply waits for a fastball, which he rockets for a double.

4. A left-handed hitter wants to put down a bunt. He knows that the element of surprise will be greater if he waits until the count is 2-0. Sure enough, on that count, he gets a fastball and puts down an excellent bunt that catches the third baseman by surprise.

Becoming a smart hitter stems mostly from simple experience. In other words, few Little Leaguers would notice these nuances, and even high school players wouldn't often notice these things. But in college and pro ball, they are essential components of the inner world of baseball.

To educate yourself about these subtle parts of hitting, the best approach is to scrutinize the events in a major-league game. When you watch a game on television or at the ballpark, don't watch it casually. Put yourself in the batter's position. See what skills he brings to the plate. Ask yourself what he's trying to accomplish on every at-bat.

Learn from the pros. Wade Boggs is one of the best hitters to watch.

© Anthony Neste

Watch Kenny Lofton hit. Will he bunt? Hit for power? Try to get a walk? Or just hit away? Observe Tony Gwynn, who knows precisely how he is going to swing at every pitch. Study Wade Boggs when he is batting. Will he slap the ball to left for a hit, or will he pull it? Watch Lance Johnson hit. Will he bunt? Take a pitch? Swing for a homer?

Find a batter you can pattern yourself after and watch him carefully. Make mental notes about what he does to succeed in the batter's box.

A FINAL WORD

Hitting is hard. Real hard. Everybody in baseball knows that. It's a fact. Accept it.

Of course, you'll still want to become the best hitter you can be. Remember these recommendations about hitting:

1. Know your strengths and your liabilities.
2. Visualize what you want to accomplish in each game. Have a precise game plan.
3. Keep your emotions in check. Too much emotion will mess up your stroke.
4. Be able to determine whether you had a quality at-bat.

Above all, have the courage to press on. Remember, in baseball, there's always tomorrow.

9

SHOWCASING YOUR SKILLS AND ATTITUDE

© Terry Wild Studio

OK, you've done it. You've followed every bit of advice in this book, worked your tail off, and now you're ready to show the baseball world that you're the real deal—the next Cal Ripken Jr. or Greg Maddux.

Terrific. Now, where do you go from here?

Sure, you've heard the stories about how a scout made a wrong turn down a dusty road in Backwater, United States, came across a sandlot game, discovered unknown Superstar, and signed him on the spot to a major-league contract.

That's the Hollywood version. True, perhaps a few players were signed in that storybook fashion. But in the real world, the way that big-league scouts "discover" you is a bit more sophisticated. Likewise, you need to know how to market yourself. The smart ballplayers, who take their game and their future in baseball seriously, do just that.

GO FOR IT! CHASE YOUR DREAMS!

Above all, remember this about being a baseball player: You have only a limited number of years in which to shine and show your stuff. The average major-league player, it's said, reaches his top physical condition between the ages of 26 and 29. After that, the wear and tear of playing begins to take effect. Of course, this presumes that you have the chance to keep playing into your late 20s. You've probably already heard that most scouts like to sign prospects when they're relatively young—just out of high school (age 18), and usually no later than age 21 or 22.

Some scouts figure that if you haven't played pro ball by the time you're 22 or 23, then you're just too old to make it as a prospect. That may sound harsh, but there's enough evidence to show that by the time you're 23, you should be on your way to the big leagues; otherwise, the odds are stacked monumentally against you.

Ironically, in most careers, a young person of 21 or 22 is considered just a kid—someone who's just starting out in the business. But in the world of pro baseball, a player of 22 is considered to be gaining on middle age.

Think about your development as a ballplayer in terms of a ticking clock. You have just so many years, a finite amount of time, to develop your skills before the clock runs out. From the time you first pick up a bat and ball as a five-year-old, the clock starts ticking. It will keep on ticking, even while your desire, determination, and physical abilities keep pushing you ahead in the game.

That's why it's so important to start developing your skills in your teen years. If you wait until you're 24 or 25, there's little chance you'll play pro ball. Look at the roster of any major-league club. There might be a few veteran players, but most teams have players who are in their mid-20s. If you look at minor-league rosters, you'll find that the ages are even younger.

So if your dream is to become the best ballplayer you can be, my advice is to start young and go for it now. Set your sights on what you want to improve in your game, and just do it. Don't let grouchy or negative coaches get in the way of your enthusiasm or excitement. The world is chock-full of players who overcame the odds to become star athletes.

WHAT SCOUTS LOOK FOR IN A PROSPECT

Before you can try to impress the scouts, you must figure out what they're looking for. And trust me—scouting young ballplayers is a tough job.

First off, consider that scouts see literally hundreds of young ballplayers each spring and summer. On a typical day a scout might see three or four high school or college games. That means he might stay at one game for three innings, leave to find another game and watch two innings there, and so on. Sometimes, a scout may only watch infield and outfield practice before leaving.

The reality is that there are many ballplayers and only a handful of scouts. And you never know when a scout is watching one of your games; after all, they rarely run out on the field and introduce themselves!

So the first advice is simple. Because you don't know when a scout is at your game, just assume that he's always there. Dress, play, and hustle accordingly. Assume otherwise and you could cut your chances dramatically. After all, scouts aren't too thrilled about recommending that a kid be signed if he doesn't hustle on the field, lets his uniform shirt hang out, or argues with the umpire. So when you take the field, look and act like a pro. You'll be surprised how few of your teammates or opponents do this simple task.

WHERE DO SCOUTS FIND PROSPECTS?

Good question. Common sense tells you that you have a much better chance of being seen and scouted if you play for a team (or in a league) that is frequented by scouts. To find out which teams these are, ask around. Ask your coach. Ask local umpires. Find out about all-star tournaments and open tryouts in your area. Ask the sportswriter from the local paper. Ask older kids who are serious players. Look in the local newspaper for reports about good teams and leagues.

Don't wait for those teams to come to you. Many youngsters make that mistake. Get on the phone and do some work. Remember, the more calls and the more homework you do, the more informed you'll be as a player.

EVALUATING A PROSPECT

Traditionally, a scout evaluates a player along five lines:

Hitting

This is the player's ability to hit a ball consistently well against top amateur pitching. The ball jumping off the bat indicates that the prospect has excellent bat speed and strong wrists.

Hitting With Power

Contrary to popular belief, this is not necessarily the ability of the hitter to slug a pitch a long ways. Rather, it's the ability to hit the ball hard (as well as far) and consistently against top pitching.

Running Speed

Pure running speed is what the scouts look for first, but they also notice an instinctive ability to run the bases, get a good jump, steal, and take the extra base.

Fielding

Soft hands, excellent range, and an ability to make both the routine and the extraordinary play are the qualities of a good defensive player. Heads-up play in the field is also important.

Arm Strength

A player with a good arm has power and velocity on his throws, along with accuracy and an instinctive knowledge of where to throw the ball. But lest you think that scouting is a simple process, read on. It's not simple at all.

When scouts evaluate a player, they make two evaluations. The first one rates the player as a player today. The second evaluation is how the scout feels the player is going to develop over the next few years. There's a major difference—and this two-step scouting process is something the vast majority of high school coaches and parents aren't aware of.

Let's assume you're an 18-year-old high school shortstop and pitcher. When the scout evaluates your play, he's going to compare you not with your teammates or opponents but with current major leaguers. That may sound a bit harsh. After all, how many 18-year-olds compare favorably to major leaguers? But that's not the point. What the scout is doing is applying a standard measure of comparison that's known to other scouts in his organization. That way scouts can compare and contrast high school prospects from all over the country.

The second part of the evaluation is even trickier. In this evaluation, the scout uses his years of experience to predict how much better a ballplayer you'll become as you get older. He must consider many factors: how much bigger you're going to get, how much stronger, how much faster, and so on. In many ways, this is the real test of scouting—trying to predict the future of a young man.

Big-league scouts commonly use a scale of 20 to 80 to evaluate prospects, with 50 representing an average major leaguer's skills. Keep in mind that an average major leaguer is a heckuva great ballplayer; after all, less than 800 men are playing in the big leagues at any one time, and to be average in the big leagues is a major accomplishment. After all, an "average" major leaguer makes well over a million dollars a year!

So let's say you're a decent high school ballplayer, and the scout marks you down as being in the low 40s and high 30s for your running, hitting, hitting with power, fielding, and arm strength. Off the top of your head, you might think that your

SCOUT'S RATING CARD

Rating key

80–Outstanding	60–Above average	40–Below average	20–Poor
70–Very good	50–Average	30–Well below average	

Position player

Position player	Present	Future	Use rating key grades — Show times to first and dashes					
Hitting	_____	_____	Hitch	____	Bat speed	____	Contact	____
Power	_____	_____	Pull	____	Alley	____	Line drive	____
Speed	_____	_____	To first base	____	40-yd dash	____	60-yd dash	____
Arm	_____	_____	Strength	____	Accuracy	____	Release	____
Field	_____	_____	Range	____	Hands	____	Agility	____
Base running	_____	_____	Instincts	____	Aggressiveness	____	Leads	____

Type of hitter (circle proper category)   Power   Line drive   Slap

Player's makeup

Competitiveness _____		Intelligence _____	
Confidence _____		Poise _____	
Dependability _____		Teamwork _____	
Honesty _____			

Pitcher

Pitcher	Present	Future	Use rating key grades			
Fastball	_____	_____	Velocity (mph) ____	Life	____
Curve	_____	_____	Velocity ____	Break	____
Slider	_____	_____	Velocity ____	Break	____
Change	_____	_____	Fastball ____	Breaking pitch	____
Other pitch	_____	_____	Type ____	Control	____
Control	_____	_____	Fastball ____	Breaking ball	____

Type of pitcher (circle proper category)   Power   Sink/slide   Finesse

Player's makeup

Competitiveness _____		Intelligence _____	
Confidence _____		Poise _____	
Dependability _____		Teamwork _____	
Honesty _____			

Explanation and Formula for Grading

In arriving at the total grade, use only the future grades. The formula is different for the position player than for the pitcher.

For the position player you total five boxes: hitting, power, speed, arm, and fielding. Take the total of the five boxes and divide by 5.

For the pitcher, you total at the most five boxes: fastball, curve, slider, other pitch, and control. I the pitcher only shows you a fastball and curve, then you total these two plus control for three boxes. In any case, you only divide the totl by the number of boxes you graded him in, and never by any more than 5.

In completing the formula, you may either upgrade or downgrade the grade after division, by anywhere from 1 to 4 points.

Example:

Position player

Ability	Present	Future
Hitting	33	47
Power	43	52
Speed	61	72
Arm	59	61
Field	52	69
		Total these grades only

The total of the future grades in this area is 301. Divide the total of 301 by 5. The overall grade to this point is 60.2. You may upgrade this player 3 points because of his superior makeup. Add these 3 points to the 60.2 and you get a total of 63.2.

Example:

Pitcher

Ability	Present	Future
Fastball	37	54
Curve	39	47
Slider	44	57
Other pitch	None	
Control	45	56
		Total these grades only

Because you evaluated this pitcher in four categories, then you divide by 4. The total of the future grades in this area is 214. Divide the total of 214 by 4. The overall grade to this point is 53.5.

Because of his makeup, you my downgrade this pitcher 3 points. Subtract these 3 points from the 53.5, and you get a total of 50.5.

Reprinted, by permission, from A. Goldis and R. Wolff, 1988, *Breaking into the big leagues: How to make pro scouts notice you* (Champaign, IL: Human Kinetics), 60-61.

scores are very poor. In reality, they're outstanding because your current abilities are being compared to current major leaguers. Most high school players score in the 20s if they score at all.

Let's also say that the scout sees you five years down the road as having abilities in the 50s and 60s. Well, with those kinds of scores, it would be a rare scout who didn't offer you a bonus contract on the spot. After all, he's predicting that by the time you're 23 you'll be as good as, or better than, the average major leaguer.

How many of these good scores do you need? Well, if you score well on just three, you become a prospect. For example, let's say you're a middle infielder. You're of average size. With the glove, you're sensational. Your arm is strong when throwing to first. You run much better than average, almost exceptionally fast. These components make you a bona fide prospect, as the scouts would say.

But let's keep going. Unfortunately, you don't hit for much power. And in terms of general hitting, well, you're good, but not great.

Here's the bottom line. Of the five key components, you project well on three. That's good. If your hitting improves, you would grade out well on four of the five elements, making you a top prospect.

How about some real-life examples? Staying with middle infielders, think of Ozzie Smith. When Smith signed a pro contract out of Cal Poly San Luis Obispo, the scouts could see that he had great ability with the glove, that he had a strong arm, and that he had outstanding speed.

Was Ozzie a premier, "can't miss" hitter? Well, quite honestly, no. Sure, he was good for college ball, but compared to professional hitters his hitting was not a strength. And hitting for power? Well, again, that's not Ozzie's strength.

But the scouts recognized that Ozzie possessed three key tools necessary to become a decent shortstop at the major-league level, and he got a chance. He became the game's top defensive shortstop and along the way, he became a fairly decent hitter—all through hard work. That's how he became an all-star shortstop destined for the Hall of Fame.

WHAT NOT TO SHOW THE SCOUTS

Here are a few surefire ways to get the pro scouts to cross your name off their list of prospects:

1. Act like a hot dog on the field. Show off. Show up your opponents, your coach, or the umpire. Nobody wants a player with an attitude problem.

2. Act as if you don't care much about your appearance. Wear your uniform in a sloppy manner and maintain a disheveled demeanor to tip off scouts that you don't aspire to a professional contract.

3. Play when you're really hurt or when you have a sore arm. While it may be valiant, it doesn't let the scout get an accurate idea of how you can play.

4. Act as if you're bored with the action on the field. This tells the scout that you'd rather be someplace other than the ballfield.

5. Be unfamiliar with the rules of the game. That's always a sign to a scout that you don't take the game seriously. Not running hard when there are two outs or not knowing about the infield-fly rule will make it easy for the scout to make an unfavorable recommendation.

HOW GOOD DO YOU HAVE TO BE?

Before you start dreaming about how you're going to spend your bonus money, keep a few realities in mind. Being graded and projected by the scouts is very competitive. There are literally tens of thousands of young ballplayers in the world, and chances are that many of them can do most of the things you can do. What the scout is looking for is that exceptional player who sparkles in the field, runs like the wind, and hits like Ken Griffey Jr. or Frank Thomas. Or at least plays as if he might someday be that good.

Consider that out of the millions of kids who have played baseball over the last century, only about 13,500 have ever played in the major leagues. Now, I don't know what percentage that is, but it's pretty slim.

Do your own scouting reports. Look at a typical major-league lineup. Most major-league ballclubs have one or two superstars (players who rate highly on several offensive skills), but the rest of the lineup is usually filled out with players who have only a couple outstanding abilities.

Let's look at a typical Cleveland Indians lineup from the 1995 season. Leading off is Ken Lofton, a bona fide superstar. Kenny can hit, hit with power occasionally, has great speed, is a marvelous center fielder, and has an average arm. So of the five categories, Lofton ranks with the best in at least three.

The number-two hitter is Omar Vizquel. Omar is a Gold Glove shortstop but only an average major-league hitter, with little power and so-so speed. Carlos Baerga, who bats third, is a fine hitter with pop in his bat, but is below average defensively and doesn't run well. Albert Belle follows. Albert has great hitting ability and great power. But he has only average foot speed and is weak defensively, with both his glove and his arm.

In any event, you get the idea. It's extremely rare to find a player—even in the major leagues—who rates highly in all five

It's rare to find a player in the major leagues who rates highly all around. Carlos Baerga is a fine hitter with a clean stroke, but is below average defensively.

© VJ Sports Photography

categories. When you start developing the ability to rate players, you begin to understand how the scouts look at you.

Of course, many players made it to the minors before realizing that they weren't going to go any further. Among the more notable former minor leaguers are the former governor of New York Mario Cuomo, musician-singer Charley Pride, wrestler Randy "Wild Man" Savage, football analyst John Dockery, college basketball coach Tom Penders, and many others, including NBA player Michael Jordan.

All scouts will tell you that projecting players into the future is not a science. Major-league general managers claim that for every 20 ballplayers signed to a professional contract (Rookie ball to Class AAA), only 2 or 3 will ever reach the big leagues, even for a day. Yes, it's that competitive.

Yet every year you'll hear stories of ballplayers who weren't chosen in the annual June draft but somehow got to the major leagues. You'd be surprised at how many name players weren't drafted. Scouts cast off these players as being not talented enough. Perhaps the scouts didn't see them enough, or somehow they fell through the cracks.

Mike Lansing, one of the top infielders in the National League, is a typical case. Lansing played for Wichita State and was ready for pro ball in 1990. The only pro team that showed any interest in Mike was a Class A independent team, the Miami Miracle. Lansing was understandably disappointed that no other pro club was interested in his services, but he was grateful for the chance with Miami. He signed and played two years for the ballclub.

In a typical baseball way, Felipe Alou, now the manager of the Expos but then the manager of the West Palm Beach Expos in the Florida State League, saw and liked Mike's play. Alou recommended to the Montreal front office that they buy Lansing's contract from the Miami Miracle. That's how Lansing got into Montreal's system. Every other major-league team saw, and passed, on Lansing when he was in high school and college. Yet Mike held fast to his dream, and eventually it came true.

Consider also that players like Don Mattingly were relatively low draft choices. Mattingly was taken in the 16th round. Ryne Sandberg was drafted in the 21st round. Keith Hernandez wasn't drafted until the 42nd round. And Dodgers all-star Mike Piazza wasn't selected until the 60th round!

Piazza is an interesting story, too, because when he was drafted, it was done mostly as a favor by Tommy Lasorda to Piazza's dad, a close friend. The Dodgers didn't think Mike was much of a prospect. But all Mike wanted was a chance, and he eventually worked his way through the minor-league system to the bigs.

Mike Piazza was one of many late-round draft choices who's become a star.

THE IMPACT OF DESIRE

You've heard it a zillion times from your Little League coaches on up, but it remains true: While most young ballplayers dream about playing pro ball, only a handful ever really put the effort into making the grade.

You see, as you progress from high school into the college ranks, pure, raw talent carries you only so far. After talent, the only factor you can control is your determination to keep progressing. Baseball is like any other skill in life: The more you practice it, the better you become. But according to most studies, the vast majority of aspiring ballplayers give up the sport around high school age, because the game becomes too tough, or because other activities in life become more important, or because the player doesn't want to pay the price to keep working at a very difficult game. And there's no question about it—baseball becomes a tougher game as you go up the ladder.

THE KEY TO SUCCESS

Let's assume, though, that you do have some talent and you don't mind paying the price of hard work and long hours. What, then, separates you from the rest?

According to my experience as a coach in college and pro ball, the big key for the young player is to gain a sense of awareness of himself. That means you must start objectively analyzing your abilities on the ballfield and learn how to maximize those skills.

It also means that if you aren't having success at a certain level, then you must have the courage to experiment and try new approaches. But trying new approaches doesn't mean just taking a few extra swings or fooling around in the bullpen with a new pitch. It means taking a step back, carefully analyzing what is working for you (and even more important, what *isn't* working for you), and then planning your new strategy.

This kind of self-assessment is routine with professional players; they do it all the time. One example of a player who had the courage to reevaluate himself and make the necessary transformation is Greg McMichael, the fine relief pitcher for the Atlanta Braves.

Greg was pitching for Cleveland's Class AAA team in the early 1990s, and just wasn't getting the job done. So he was released (baseball's term for being fired). But Greg was determined and still wanted to pitch. He believed in himself, and more important, he thought he could reevaluate why he wasn't making progress to the majors. He decided that what he needed was another pitch, and in his case, the best bet was a change-up.

As it developed, Greg had a difficult time getting another chance. But he eventually hooked on with the Braves. They sent him back down the ladder to a Class A team, where he started to work on that new pitch—the change-up. He kept working at that pitch, and thanks to his courageous self-assessment, Greg eventually got to the show with the Braves. He has been a stellar performer ever since.

IMPROVE YOUR CHANCES

More important than anything, you have to play the game. Parents and kids ask me all the time, "Is it better to be a second-string player on a talented team, or is it better to be the star on a weak team?" To me, there's no debate on this one. Quite simply, you don't get any better watching someone else play. Above all else, you've got to play!

It doesn't matter what position you play when you're just starting out in high school. Let's assume you're an infielder, and you're only a sophomore. You're good as an infielder, but several seniors who are returning to the team are also infielders. Your best bet is to tell the coach that you prefer playing infield, but for the sake of making the team, you'll try the outfield. Again, it doesn't matter where you play, as long as you play.

What about college? If you really want to play ball in college, you should ask the college coach two questions: Who played my position for you last year? What year in school is he? If you're a third baseman, and the college's third baseman was a star player this year as a freshman, then you should realize that you're going to have an uphill battle for the next three years trying to beat this guy out of the lineup.

Now, I'm not suggesting that you should not attend a college merely because there's a kid ahead of you on the baseball team's depth chart; after all, star players do become injured, transfer, or sometimes just play poorly. Besides, you may be a better player than the kid ahead of you. My point is that you should do your homework first and know precisely what's ahead of you before you commit yourself to four years at a particular college. Yes, kids do transfer from college to college, but doing a little homework now can save you headaches down the road.

QUESTIONS TO ASK COLLEGE COACHES

First off, you should know that if you plan to play ball in college, there's a tremendous amount of confusion about the levels of competition among colleges and universities.

While in college football it's pretty clear that a Division I team would beat up on a Division III school, that's not always true in college baseball. It would take an entire book to explain just this one point, but the truth is that many colleges listed as Division I in baseball have relatively weak programs. Similarly, there are Division II and III colleges that are absolute power- houses in baseball, and these schools could easily handle major Division I competition.

For example, when I coached at Mercy College (a Division II school in Dobbs Ferry, New York), we had at least eight full athletic scholarships to hand out in baseball. I did a great deal of recruiting, and because I was able to offer baseball scholar- ships, I attracted some great players to the Mercy program. We routinely played Division I schools that had no baseball scholarships to offer, and usually Mercy would win big. The casual observer would say, "How about that? A Division II college just rolled over a Division I program."

During my tenure at Mercy, it was also clear to me that the Division III state schools in New Jersey were perennial power- houses. Under NCAA rules and regulations, a Division III program can't offer any athletic scholarships. But these New Jersey state universities had dynamite, big-time programs. They were Division III in name only; in terms of talent, they were big time.

So you have to do your homework when it comes to planning for college. Start early. Ask around. Ask your high school coach about various college programs. Ask your summer league coaches. Ask your high school guidance counselor. Most important, write or call the college coaches yourself.

When writing a professional letter, address the college coach by name. Introduce yourself to him, tell him of your interest in his program, and ask if there are any brochures or materials he can send you about the program. Also ask if there is any way you can come to visit the college and him.

Don't wait until the spring of your senior year to write these letters; write them in early autumn of your senior year. If you don't hear from the coach after a few weeks, call him directly (or have your school guidance counselor call him).

Be certain to include your stats as a ballplayer and your academic record. Remember, college coaches beat the bushes looking for prospects. You're doing him a service by letting him know about you and your talents. Believe me, most college coaches respond quickly to these kinds of letters. If you have a decent video of yourself in action, send a copy (not your only copy!) to the coach. Put your name on it, make certain you identify yourself to the coach on the tape, and keep the tape relatively brief—no more than five or six minutes.

Continue to ask around about college programs. Sure, everybody knows about the programs at Miami and Stanford. They're at the top of the list. But how good is the Wisconsin at Oshkosh program? What about Adelphi University in New York? How good is Elon College in North Carolina? You may not have heard of these fine colleges, but all three have great baseball programs.

Currently more than three thousand colleges and universities in the United States offer baseball programs. Thousands of junior colleges do as well. Every year, coaches at each of those colleges must find new and talented players. So, set aside a few days during the beginning of your senior year and start mapping out your next step in academics and in baseball. It will be time well spent.

SCOUTS AND PRO BALL

Don't wait for scouts to find you. Go and find them. More precisely, make certain you get into a competitive league where scouts routinely come to watch games.

By the time you're a junior or senior in high school or college, playing in a summer league that isn't scouted won't advance your baseball career. You could be the next Manny Ramirez, but if no scout is watching, you might as well be invisible.

Think of getting a job in baseball as your first attempt at marketing yourself to the real world. Check out the leagues. Ask around. Find out where the scouts *do* show up. Then make every effort to get yourself into that league as a player.

KNOW WHERE TO LOOK

To get the inside track on where to find scouts, subscribe to the key publications in the baseball world. That would include *Baseball America, Collegiate Baseball,* and *USA Today Baseball Weekly.* If you read those publications on a regular basis, you'll learn where the best amateur leagues are, where baseball clinics are being given in your area, and all sorts of inside information about how and where to pursue a baseball career. Read beyond the standard baseball stories. Take time to peruse the various advertisements and other announcements that routinely appear in these papers.

The dedicated ballplayer will find these publications invaluable. All three sell at newsstands around the country; you can, of course, subscribe. Also, most major libraries carry these publications in their standard reference section.

Finally, I strongly urge you to purchase a copy of Baseball America's annual *Directory.* It's a complete listing of every person in every organization, plus a listing of every Division I baseball program in the country, with phone numbers, addresses, and so on. Believe me, everybody in pro ball has this publication. It's on sale everywhere each spring. Don't forget to contact the NCAA in Kansas for any questions or information you may need about college programs—Divisions I, II, or III, or junior college. Call them directly at 1-913-339-1906.

SHOWCASE YOUR TALENT

One of the best features of these publications is that they include information about local showcase tournaments. These showcase tournaments, such as the baseball Area Code

Tournaments, have become immensely popular in recent years in amateur baseball, especially for high school players.

Local scouts flock to these events because they provide an opportunity to see the best kids in their area play ball. The tournaments are usually publicized in *Collegiate Baseball* and *Baseball America,* but to get more information, check with your high school or summer-league coach. Don't wait until the last minute to do so.

A WORD ON TRYOUT CAMPS

Professional scouts run two basic types of tryout camps—open and closed. An open tryout is just that—it's open to anyone and everyone. Usually these are well publicized in your area, and every ballplayer who has aspirations of being signed shows up to try out.

Because so many kids show up, these open tryouts can last for hours. They usually start at 9 A.M. and last through 6 P.M., sometimes later. Ballplayers first have to fill out some paperwork. Next, they're usually timed in 60-yard dashes, given infield or outfield drills, and then given some batting practice against live pitching.

If the tryout attracts hundreds of players, and only a couple of scouts are running it, you can see that there's going to be a lot of waiting around. My advice is that you go (especially if you haven't been to many tryouts in the past) but be aware that it's going to be a long day. Take a lunch with you and plenty to drink in case it's warm.

Is an open tryout worth it? Yes! If nothing else, the scout has a chance to meet you, see you in action, and most important, add you to his follow-up list. Getting on the scout's follow-up list is essential because it might get you invited to a closed tryout.

A closed tryout is even better. These are by invitation only. Scouts usually invite only a dozen or so players, all of whom are considered serious prospects. If you receive an invitation to one of these sessions, you must already realize you're a pretty good player.

In any event, because there are only a relative handful of players at a closed tryout, the session is much shorter. You'll be asked to go through many of the same drills as before, but here you'll get the full attention of the scouts in attendance. During a closed tryout, of course, you want to put forth your finest effort.

INDEPENDENT PROFESSIONAL LEAGUES

Just a few years ago, there weren't many places to play pro ball unless you were signed to a contract by one of the major-league organizations. But in the 1990s, thanks to the resurgence in popularity of minor-league baseball, new professional leagues have been popping up all over the map.

True, some of these new independent leagues haven't made it. But many of them have not only survived, they've thrived. Perhaps the best known of these leagues is the Northern League, founded by Miles Wolff. While the Northern League and others like it don't have any affiliation with major-league teams, they offer great opportunities for young ballplayers: (1) you get a chance to showcase your talents in a pro setting; (2) a major-league team might purchase your contract because many scouts watch these games; and (3) you're playing baseball all summer and being paid for it. It's a combination that's hard to beat. Don't forget the Mike Lansing story!

BASEBALL CAREERS OVERSEAS

Back in the 1980s, the idea of playing pro baseball in a country outside North America was still on the far horizon. It was something that might happen someday.

Well, that day has arrived. You probably already know that baseball is indeed a global sport, played in more than one hundred countries around the world. Besides the top professional leagues in Japan and Australia, professional leagues are also springing up in Korea, China, the Netherlands, Italy, Cuba, Brazil, and South Africa, to name just a few. According to Major League Baseball International, the growth of the sport continues on a yearly basis.

It is now routine for athletes who learned to play baseball in faraway countries to come to the United States and become stars. Players like Dave Nilsson, Graeme Lloyd, and Craig

Shipley were born and raised in Australia. Hideo Nomo, of course, is Japanese, and Chan Ho Park is Korean. And many bright stars are playing in the minors, like pitcher Jose Pett, who was born and raised in Brazil.

© Anthony Neste

Baseball is international. Hideo Nomo left Japan and made his debut in major-league baseball in 1995.

As the sport spreads around the world, more opportunities to play in these countries are opening up. To get more information, contact Major League Baseball International in New York City or subscribe to *International Rundown,* the leading publication on what is happening in international baseball. It's worth getting and it's fun to read (the last issue I received included an article about the growth of baseball in Mongolia!).

The idea of some day having a true World Series—in which the best teams from all over the world compete—is no longer just a pipe dream. It will definitely happen in your lifetime.

IN SUM

Baseball is a great game, and as it expands worldwide, it's becoming even better. Can you imagine the experience of playing in a baseball tournament in Italy? Or in South Africa? Or in Japan? These wonderful events are already happening, and their numbers will only grow in the future.

So look upon baseball as a sport in which you can chart your progress, on both a daily and yearly basis. As you climb the ladder, always remember that whether you make the big leagues or not, the enjoyment and gratification come from chasing your dreams, and from making the most of your potential.

If, at the end of your baseball career, you can honestly look back and say to yourself, "You know, I gave it everything I had," then that's all you could ask. Then it will be time to pass on your hard-earned baseball knowledge to the next generation of ballplayers.

INDEX

ABOUT THE AUTHOR

Rick Wolff's inside knowledge of baseball comes from an outstanding career as a professional player, television analyst, writer, and coach. He played in the 1971 College World Series while a sophomore at Harvard University. The following year, he was drafted by and signed with the Detroit Tigers. When his playing career ended, Wolff served for eight years as the head coach at Mercy College (NY), where he transformed a struggling Division III program into a nationally ranked Division II organization. From 1989 to 1994, Wolff served as the roving performance enhancement coach for the Cleveland Indians.

The author of 14 books about sports, business, and sport psychology, Wolff has written articles for numerous consumer and academic publications ranging from *Sports Illustrated* and *Sport* to *Psychology Today* and *Psychological Reports*. He has served as on-air commentator on ESPN, SportsChannel, and the Madison Square Garden Network.

Wolff received his undergraduate degree in psychology from Harvard University, magna cum laude, and his master's from Long Island University, with high honors. He is a long-time member of the American Baseball Coaches Association and the Association for the Advancement of Applied Sports Psychology. He lives in Armonk, NY, with his wife and three children.

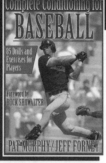